THE COMPLETE

Aspects of Love

VIKING
STUDIO
BOOKS

THE COMPLETE

Aspects of Love

KURT GÄNZL

Photographs by Clive Barda

Research by Jane Rice

Contents

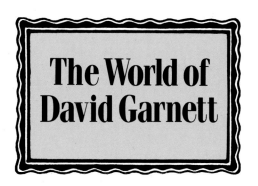

The World of David Garnett

T here was always more than an outside chance that David Garnett would end up having something to do with books. By the time he was born, in 1892, his family had already been involved, in one way or another, with different areas of the world of literature for almost a century. Even so, for quite a while it seemed as though the tradition of what had come, since his great-grandfather's day, to be looked upon virtually as the Garnett family business might be broken. In spite of a childhood passed in a home where books were the staff of life, and where many of the literary stars of the period were frequent guests, the young man's chosen education and training were certainly not what might have been expected to form a reputable novelist of the Edwardian era. Yet ultimately it was he, David, of all the respected and celebrated members of his family, who, in a career spanning more than sixty years, made the most significant mark as a creative writer.

The most prominent Garnetts of the eighteenth and early nineteenth centuries had been more inclined to profit than to poetry or prose, and they had included among their ranks some notably successful businessmen. One of these, David's uncle Jeremiah Garnett, had been involved in the founding and early direction of the *Manchester Guardian*, and was, in its early days, often to be found, pen in hand, himself contributing to his growing newspaper; but it was Jeremiah's brother, the Revd Richard Garnett, who was the first to take a definitive turn in the direction of a career in letters, thus setting the stage for his descendants' way of life throughout the next 150 years.

Thoroughly educated in the classics, in languages and in theological subjects, Richard originally took up the Church as a career and, as he rose gradually from the post of village curate to that of vicar through positions in Cleveland, Blackburn, Lichfield and Staffordshire, he found that his extensive learning allowed him to take an active part in the various, often fiery, theological debates which filled the newspapers and journals of the day.

There were plenty of opportunities for him to leap into print, since religious preoccupations and polemics of all kinds were, at that time, given a prominence in the papers which is equalled only by the sporting columns of modern times, and the

Three generations of Garnetts: Edward, David and Richard

The Revd Richard Garnett

Revd Richard Garnett soon distinguished himself in this way. Before long, he turned his attention beyond purely ecclesiastical topics. His exceptional skill in languages led him to become passionately involved in the newly distinguished science of philology and the learned arguments that it provoked, and he soon became noted as a leading authority on the structure and use of the English language. Areas of scholarly and sometimes very theoretical study such as this were, at the time, often the province of the clergy, who made up an important element of the highly educated part of the population, but Richard's specialist knowledge ultimately led him away from the Church and the provinces and into the city of London and the world of books. In 1838 he was appointed Assistant Keeper of the Department of Printed Books at the British Museum.

The department was not the British Library that we know today. The famous domed Reading Room did not exist, and there was no automatic source of, or indeed stock room for, the vast range of books nowadays supplied to the library by the country's innumerable publishers. It was a collection of more or less ancient books, many of a learned or didactic nature, mostly bequeathed or donated to the museum from collections and libraries built up by private booklovers. Some of these legacies and gifts, from extremely rich and knowledgeable men, were remarkable and already, in the early decades of the century, the Department of Printed Books housed a magnificent selection of volumes. It was in the years following Richard's arrival, however, that it began to be built into one of the world's great repositories of literature.

It cannot be said that Richard was himself in any way responsible for this. During the twelve years he spent in his position at the museum, he continued his private scholarly activities and writings, while the man who had appointed him revolutionized what was to become the British Library. Antonio Panizzi had come to England in the 1820s as a political refugee after getting a little too closely involved in revolution of a rather different kind in his native Italy, and he had risen from an assistant's position to head the Printed Books division of the museum. It was he who was responsible for the construction of the famous Reading Room, and he who reorganized the library into the basis of the world-famous collection it is today, winning wide and immediate recognition which later resulted not only in his being put at the head of the entire British Museum but also, in spite of his foreign nationality, becoming Sir Antony, KCB.

The influence of the good and great Panizzi on the destinies of the Garnett family was not limited to bringing the philological country vicar to town and to a comfortable place in the world of books. When Richard Garnett died, in 1850 at the age of sixty-one, he left behind him three young children and Panizzi, aware of the problems which would beset the fatherless family, offered the eldest son, named Richard after his father, a job as an assistant in the library.

The sixteen-year-old boy had barely attended a regular school. Like his father before him he had been educated – indeed, largely self-educated – at home. But the kind of home which the vastly knowledgeable elder Richard had provided had given the boy every chance to dip as deeply as he cared into any branch of learning he preferred; young Richard, a bright and eagerly precocious student, had enthusiastically taken advantage of the wealth of opportunities available.

His talent for languages showed that he was truly his father's son and, at an age when boys are mostly interested in games and just a little in girls, he was devouring the classic literatures of Europe. But his self-imposed studies did not stop there, for Richard the younger was interested in all kinds of subjects, academic, social and even sporting, and he was the possessor of a voracious mind which was, in later years, to make him the subject of many tall, and probably at least partly true, stories about his remarkable feats of memory.

He entered the museum at the lowest level. Slowly – dreadfully slowly, for in that world of books men mostly move on only to meet their maker – he worked his way up. First he was promoted to the position of 'placer', a job which required him to decide where on the fast-growing shelves of the library each newly acquired book should go. Since each such decision had to be made on the basis of the content of the book, the young man had to read at least part of every volume which came his way. This duty, coupled with his famous memory, laid the foundation for the encyclopaedic knowledge which was to make him a legend.

After more than twenty years' service, Richard was promoted to the post of Assistant Keeper and put in charge of the Reading Room and then, after a period in which he undertook the massive task of organizing the first printed catalogue of the library's by now huge holdings, he was finally made Keeper of Printed Books. For the last decade of his nearly fifty years among the books of the British Museum, Richard presided over the heart of the world's published literature.

During that half-century spent as a guardian of other men's works, it was inevitable that a man of Richard's broad learning would have literary contributions of his own to make, and several dozen books appeared under his name. Most were collected and selected editions of more celebrated writers' works – Shelley, Peacock, Milton and others – which he edited or introduced; some, like *On the System of Classifying Books on the Shelves Followed at the British Museum*, were strictly functional, but Richard also tried his hand at original, imaginative work. His satirical short stories in *The Twilight of the Gods and Other Tales* won praise from some much more famous writers, and he produced sufficient poetry to fill a number of volumes. The last of these was a little book of aphorisms called *De Flagello Myrteo* and subtitled 'Thoughts and Fancies on Love'. Through Richard's thoughts and fancies, often veiled in clouds of classical references and expressed in the formal, flowery style of the

Dr Richard Garnett, 1895, by E. M. Heath

time, a picture emerges of a Victorian man who was equally at home in the domain of the heart and of the passions as he was in those of the head and of learning. And some of those thoughts and fancies are not so very different from those which, fifty years later, fascinated his grandson and – in a generation which did not have any use for coy Latin titles – became the basic themes of the more simply named *Aspects of Love*.

Richard's personal life was naturally closely involved with his work. Many of the friends whom he entertained at his home were drawn from the famous and the learned whom he met among the books of the library and, in later years, he and his family occupied the house in the museum grounds reserved for the Keeper of Books. In this literature-laden and slightly other-worldly atmosphere, his wife brought up their six children, who became used to considering the august grounds of the museum as their own back garden. There are said to have been strict words once when the youngsters were caught climbing across the roof of the great building, provoking visions of them tumbling through the vast glass dome of the Reading Room on to the readers below.

The love of books and of writing continued through to the next generation. The eldest son, Robert, a lawyer and book-collector, published several works on his hobby, as well as two volumes of memoirs and translations of the works of Dumas, while his wife found success as a sensational novelist, most notably with *The Infamous John Friend*, a work which found its way many years later on to the television screen. The youngest son, Arthur, a botanist at Kew Gardens, wrote columns on garden-ing and botany, and their middle sister, Olive, devoted herself assiduously for many years to the writing of seriously conceived novels and stories, two of which achieved publication; but it was Edward, the second of Richard's sons, who was to carry on and expand the Garnett literary tradition which his father and grandfather had begun.

Edward was neither destined nor interested in the sort of fame that comes from a blazing, exciting writing talent or a well-publicized name written large across a best-selling novel or book of verse. His great function in the world of letters, like his father's and his grandfather's before him, was a supporting one – one which would bring him no glory in the eyes of the public but which could be, and in his case was, deeply import-ant and influential. Edward was a discoverer of new brilliance, the midwife of talent both young and old. More prosaically put, he was a publisher's reader.

This may sound an unglamorous role and frequently it is an ungrateful occupation, ploughing one's way through the piles of manuscripts which arrive each week on a publisher's desk, looking for that rare one which deserves real consideration. It is the reader's job to spot, among the mass of lesser efforts by famous or faded writers and the simply competent or amateur-ish works of the unknown, that rare element of real talent – even when it lies hidden underneath layers of inexperience or mis-

Edward Garnett by E.M. Heath

judgement – that can turn a work or a writer into a winner. It was a role which Edward Garnett fulfilled brilliantly and wholeheartedly. From the age of twenty, when he deliberately slipped himself out of the dreary job he had been given in the post room of the publishing firm of Unwin and into the job of junior reader, he exercised his *métier* with a never-diminishing enthusiasm and skill for some forty years. He would winkle out and foster talented writers and push forward their works with recommendations for publication, if not by the house in which he was currently employed, then by some other suitable firm.

In Edward's hands, the role of reader was more than just that of an impersonal judge with a guillotine 'yes' or 'no' to deliver on a manuscript. When the spark of an exciting talent was there in some young or inexperienced author's work, he was ready with the kind of unerringly helpful professional and artistic advice which can come from a man of critical and literary judgement who is himself not a creative artist. Time and again he hit the mark. As the writers whom he championed rose to fame, many of them still relied strongly enough on his opinions of their new works to rewrite and alter them according to his suggestions. But, as a back-room boy, his work would have been of little lasting importance had it not been for the quality of those authors. What made Edward's forty years of such value to English literature was the amazing list of great writers whom he aided and urged from success to success.

One of the first and most notable of these was Joseph Conrad. The bearded Polish sea-captain had written the novel *Almayer's Folly* based on his experiences of life at sea, and had submitted it for publication. It arrived on Edward's desk and he recognized its potential. When he met Conrad he also recognized, behind the author's bluff assertion that the book was a one-off and that he would shortly be returning to his ship, a man longing to be encouraged as a writer. Edward tactfully provided that encouragement and, throughout Conrad's career, continued to act as his *éminence grise*, appreciating and criticizing his work, suggesting alterations and improvements, and always boosting the writer's confidence by asking him for more and more books.

W. H. Hudson had put away the unpublished manuscript of his novel *Green Mansions*, but Edward's encouragement persuaded the ageing naturalist and author to let this friendly supporter of his work see, and then promote, the book which was to give Hudson his greatest success; Edward Thomas was struggling as a prose writer until Edward discerned in his style the makings of a poet; and E. M. Forster of *Passage to India* fame, John Galsworthy, author of *The Forsyte Saga*, and H. E. Bates, whose works included *Love for Lydia*, were among those who gathered not only help and encouragement, but also an enduring friendship from Edward.

There were many others. T. E. Lawrence, the celebrated 'Lawrence of Arabia', showed Edward the manuscript of his mighty *The Seven Pillars of Wisdom*, even though he claimed that he had no intention of publishing it. But he still privately asked Edward to make any cuts and alterations which he thought necessary, and sent him, for his eyes only, his notes on his time in the RAF, ultimately published after both men were dead under the title *The Mint*. With the other Lawrence, the frenetic and equally famous D.H., Edward's relationship was even more significant and, a rare thing where the volatile author of *Women in Love* and *Lady Chatterley's Lover* was concerned, comparatively long-lasting. Edward shepherded the most famous of Lawrence's earlier works through the pitfalls and prejudices that beset the progress of this author's outspokenly sexual novels, and did not give up until he had ensured their publication. Indeed, such was Lawrence's faith in the competence and knowledge of his friend and advisor, that he left to him the task of editing the original long and strong version of *Sons and Lovers* into its final published form without even demanding to see the altered text before it was printed. Their association faded only when the temperamental Lawrence privately realized that it was developing into what to him was an unbearable dependence on the man who had become very much more than a midwife to his books.

Since Edward's reading assignments did not require him to base himself in an office, he worked largely from his London flat in Pond Place, Chelsea, and from his home, The Cearne, an isolated house set among the woodlands near Limpsfield Chart in Surrey. There he shared his life with his wife, Constance, and their young son, the future author of *Aspects of Love*. The Cearne was a true hatchery of literature, for, apart from the regular visits paid there by Edward's literary associates and friends, it was also the fountainhead of another important contribution to English literature, the pioneering work of Constance Garnett in the translation of the most significant authors of modern Russian literature.

Constance was an outstanding Victorian woman. She came from an educated family – indeed, both her parents had translated foreign works into English – but she herself had had a particularly brilliant academic career at Newnham College before taking the only avenues open to an educated young woman of her time and finding work first as a governess and then among the poor of London's East End. At the same time she became an active member of the Fabian Society and was, for a period, on its executive committee.

Constance's family had had Russian connections for several generations, her grandfather having been a sea captain who had run the first regular steamboat service between Russia and Germany. Her work in the East End had also brought her into contact with the many Russian expatriates living there, but her real interest in the Russian language and its literature was sparked rather by the personably romantic group of political exiles and dashing anti-Tsarist terrorists who cut a swathe through the drawing-rooms of liberal London in the early days of her married life.

Constance Garnett by her sister, Emma
Mahomed

Both she and Edward, having deliberately distanced themselves from what they perceived as the unacceptable style of
bourgeois Edwardian life by settling at The Cearne, gave full
rein to their slightly unworldly liberalism by fervently supporting any current war or budding revolution, particularly if it
allowed them to feel prettily guilty about being British, middle-
class and able to bathe in the mixed waters of the world's literature and art which London provided. They were pro-Boer,
anti-Tsarist, pro-Armenian and harboured a mass of feelings
over the ever-vacillating wars in the Balkans. They welcomed
the exiled heroes of the various revolutionary movements into
their home without perhaps fully understanding that some of
these were not just literary theorists and political philosophers,
but activists and even murderers.

During her pregnancy, Constance whiled away her time
teaching herself Russian, and during the difficult recovery
period following the birth of her son, she made her first
attempts at translating, under the helpful guidance and
encouragement of some of her new friends. When her first finished work was quickly accepted for publication, commissions
for further works started to come in. It was the beginning of a
career which was to occupy her for the rest of her life. Although
some translations of the more important modern Russian
works of literature had been introduced into Britain over the
previous twenty or thirty years, many of them were sub-
standard or inaccurately made from other translations rather
than from the original Russian, while others simply did not succeed in making the pieces appealing to the English public.
Equally, there were major areas which had been totally
ignored.

In thirty-five years of continuous work, and in spite of a
gradual personal disillusionment with the Bolsheviks and the
Russian Revolution, Constance filled the most important
remaining gaps and produced definitive and readable versions
not only of these unfamiliar pieces but of other works which had
not previously caught on. She brought out English versions of
the works of Turgenev, Tolstoy, Ostrovsky, Gogol and, most
notably, the first reliable translations of the works of Dostoev-
sky – *The Brothers Karamazov, The Idiot, The House of the Dead* and
Crime and Punishment among them – and the stories and plays of
Chekhov, introducing the English-speaking world to *The Cherry
Orchard, The Three Sisters* and *The Seagull.*

In the face of many newer translations of the same works,
made as the importance of, and fashion for, Russian literature
was established, much of Constance's work has been super-
seded. But in the first decades of the twentieth century she was
largely responsible for opening up a whole new and influential
area of the world's writing to English readers and writers, and
the temperate realism of the works of writers such as Chekhov
had a decided effect on novel- and play-writing in an England
still attached to Victorian styles and subjects.

* * *

David Garnett was born in 1892 into this unconventional home, this pot-pourri of variegated literary activity and odd social and anti-social influences and values. As a child he found that his friends and companions included not only local boys and girls of his own age, but a colourful collection of his father's and mother's friends and protégés, ranging from famous or soon-to-be-famous writers to dramatically discontented foreigners from whichever area of the world was currently in need of liberation from its previous group of discontented foreigners.

The youngster, who had no intention of being either a writer or a revolutionary, took it all in his stride. As an old man, he looked happily back on those years and described in his books of autobiography the memories of a make-believe ship fashioned from a washing basket and a sheet, piloted by no less a captain than Joseph Conrad; rambles through the woods and the oily waters of a local pond in search of a special species of toad in the company of W. H. Hudson; fishing with Edward Thomas; being rescued from an attack by a mad cat by Jack Galsworthy; and watching Ford Madox Ford show off his ability to twitch each of his ears, one at a time.

All this was much more important to the boy than the fact that he was spending his time with some of the best and most celebrated authors of the day. Writing was nothing special, so why should writers be? It was something which was a part of his daily life, for Constance spent many hours of most days sitting at her little table filling leaf after leaf with the results of her latest translation, letting each completed page fall to the ground alongside her in a dishevelled heap. Meanwhile Edward, with a pile of manuscripts to hand, would sit for hours on end, often till the small hours of the morning, if not actually writing himself then reviewing and correcting the work of others. Years later, describing Edward Thomas, David reminisced:

> I felt no deference or respect for authors. My friend was a hack writer like most other people I knew. I respected Conrad because he had been the captain of a sailing ship, Hudson because he knew every bird by sight and by its song, [H.W.] Nevinson and [H.N.] Brailsford because they had fought for the Greeks against the Turks – but nobody for being a writer. I either enjoyed a book a man wrote, or I did not. But I felt no more awe or respect than I did for a blackbird because I loved its song, or contempt than I did for a jay because it screeched.
>
> *Great Friends*

Whether his author friends and acquaintances impressed the boy or not, their books naturally became part of his life. Conrad sent him *The Last of the Mohicans* and Hudson a copy of his own *British Birds*, but young David was not impressed with J. M. Barrie's *The Little White Bird* and returned it to the giver with a written criticism. Like his father and his grandfather, he drew much of his education from literature read in his own home, for his formal education was both spasmodic and very

Constance Garnett and the young David

14

definitely lacking in any distinction. His favourite study, however, came less from books than from the countryside surrounding The Cearne. David was fascinated by nature and, from an early age, developed a wide and serious naturalist's knowledge of the British countryside and its wild life. His discovery of a very small but previously unidentified species of mushroom even resulted in his name becoming part of its Latin description.

His time at school was what can most kindly be called unsuccessful, and his response to the traditional English education was alarming – 'it was numbing my faculties'. He could see no reason for the existence of mathematics and his cavalier attitude to the complexities of the English language, which had been his great-grandfather's care, brought him dangerously near to failing his school exams. More disturbingly, if he showed no signs in these formative years of following in the literary part of his parents' life, he soon showed that he was ready to imitate their championing of the liberators of the world in the most desperately practical way.

While cramming for his matriculation exams, David became friendly with a Bengali student and, through him, got involved with a group of Indian would-be terrorists. When one of this amateurish team succeeded in murdering a fairly harmless diplomat, the police quickly found their way to the ringleader of the cell and, while the murderer headed on his way to the gallows, they held the rather more dangerous man who was what little brains the group possessed, while they sought a legal way of extraditing him to India. Eighteen-year-old David was determined to help him escape and, having set up an elaborate international plan, owing not a little to the colourful novels of John Buchan, set off across the Channel, in the most romantic spy fiction way, to put his plot into action. Fortunately, bad weather and treachery inside the group led to the scheme falling apart, but the young man had played his part with the utmost sincerity, and only when it was over did he see how he had been used. Liberators no longer had quite the same attraction for him after that.

The dreaded English examination somehow passed, it was time for David to begin working seriously towards the career in botany on which he had decided, and he was duly enrolled at the Imperial College of Science in South Kensington where he was to study for the next four years. He marked what he intended to be his independence and a determined step away from the world of literature and liberators by buying himself a bowler hat. Edward would never have owned a bowler hat, but David was going to dress just like his fellow students and to behave like them. He was going to be a part of the ordinary, conventional world of which he had had, up until now, little experience.

It was a brave and bold attempt, but it was rather like climbing a gravel slope – one step upwards, and two down. Too much of his time had been spent in that relaxing and self-

David Garnett by Dora Carrington

Vanessa Bell, *c.* 1918, by Duncan Grant

Lytton Strachey, 1913, by Duncan Grant

indulgent world of the simple, non-conforming way of life so unostentatiously practised by his parents and friends for him to give it all up for social conformity in one grand gesture. A man with a bowler hat did not take tea with Rupert Brooke and Dudley Ward, dance at a Women's Suffrage Ball in the garb of a Rajput prince, or tread the roads of the more romantic parts of the Continent in the company of D. H. Lawrence and his wife, the dangerously hedonistic Frieda. A man with a bowler hat did not associate with the suspiciously amoral folk who gathered around the young members of the Stephen family and their Cambridge University friends, who had set up house in Bloomsbury with the avowed aim of living their lives in their own way, uninhibited by convention and their parents. But David did.

Friendship with Adrian Stephen brought him to the fringe of what would later be known as the Bloomsbury Group and he was dazzled by this, his own personal discovery of a group of 'beautiful people' – Adrian, his sisters Virginia and Vanessa (soon to be famous by the names of their husbands, Leonard Woolf and Clive Bell), the painter Duncan Grant, economist Maynard Keynes, author Lytton Strachey and others, less talented but of like mind and moral attitude, who followed them.

> During my visits I felt a strange mixture of emotions: the excitement of meeting people who were more charming and more intelligent than the people I met elsewhere – and a feeling of peacefulness, of being at home – almost a premonition of belonging, as though I were some stray kitten which had firmly made up its mind that it was going to be adopted.
>
> *Golden Echo*

Having made up his mind as to what he wanted, David worked at being accepted. Cleverly and carefully the agreeable and reasonably penniless botany student made himself a cosily accepted place alongside the comparatively well-off leading members of Bloomsbury, writers and painters of a different generation from the ones with whom he had grown up and, with the exception of Virginia Woolf, Maynard Keynes and Lytton Strachey, not in the same league, but writers and painters all the same. Before long he was able to abandon the full evening dress which (it being his only respectable outfit) he had startled everyone by wearing to each Bloomsbury party, and relax in the companionship of the people he so admired.

It took little effort for him, brought up in a relaxed and liberal atmosphere by his parents, to fit in with the 'peace and love' philosophy of the Bloomsbury boys and girls and, indeed, he made a much happier job of following their professed aims of moral and sexual tolerance and freedom than many of the group's figureheads whose lives and love affairs, heterosexual and homosexual, became both complicated and miserable. David, to whom love in its various shapes and styles had always been a very important part of life, later claimed to have got his ideas on love and sex thoroughly sorted out at this time:

I had, up till then, been, in my love-affairs, an unrepentant senti-
mentalist and, like most sentimentalists, an unconscious hypo-
crite... [Now I realized that sincerity was a chief virtue in love or
lust] and adopted for ever after a more honest attitude to my
amours. I became, and for the rest of my life have remained, in
what I take to be the true meaning of the word, a libertine: that is
a man whose sexual life is free of the restraints imposed by reli-
gion and conventional morality. But I am not, and had little impulse ever to become, a rake: that is a man whose loose life is the
result of a reaction against the restraints imposed by his upbring-
ing, or one who has a psychological craving for self-destruction
and seeks it in a brothel, or the gutter.

David Garnett, 1916, by Duncan Grant

Bloomsbury had apparently done its work well. A rashly
sentimental young man had grown into an uncomplicated and
complaisant lover. But if his new environment and his new
friends had sorted out that side of his life, they had not yet
encouraged him to develop an artistic or literary life. Although
he was surrounded by the various efforts of the members of
Bloomsbury, almost all of whom had ambitions as authors or
artists, more or less serious and more or less successful, he made
no attempt himself to set pen to paper. And, although he was
known to have taken up a paint brush from time to time, he did
not attempt to compete with his more serious friends in that
area either. He was still a botanist. But not for long.

The First World War put an end to David's scientific
career. Botany took a definite second place behind Bloomsbury
as, in the company of his friend Francis Birrell, he set off for
France, where the two men spent some time working on relief
programmes with the Quakers in the unoccupied zone. On his
return, he and Duncan Grant, conscientious objectors both,
went into exile together in the farmlands of Sussex, working as
labourers on a farm hastily organized by the generous Vanessa.
She was only too well aware that, in her current and intensely-
felt love affair with Grant, she was having to take second place
to an equally strong affair between the two men. In the end,
however, a few weeks after the Armistice, Vanessa gave birth to
Duncan's child – a daughter called Angelica. David smilingly
informed the parents that he would one day marry her. Twenty
years, a marriage, two sons and two careers later, he did just
that.

The first of the two careers was a four-year post-war stint in
business as a bookseller, an occupation for which he was only
slightly better suited than his partner, the charming but finan-
cially insouciant Birrell; the marriage, in 1921, was to Rachel
(Ray) Marshall and, producing both the two sons and inspiring
the second career, as a writer, it was, at least in its earlier years,
much more of a success.

David had, by now, already come round to making his first
attempts at writing, although not in any particularly ambitious
or serious way. He had, on occasions, been of help to his mother
in her work on the Russian authors, but it was David the botanist, fresh from his experiences in the Sussex fields, who first

Ray Garnett

made his way into print in 1918 with a much abridged and adapted English version of the useful but out-of-date French book on vegetable gardening, Gresset's *Le Potager Moderne*. The following year, being at a loss for some ready cash, he decided to try another stab at authorship and, this time, still nowhere near confident enough to use his own voice, he constructed instead a photofit piece of ghastly woman's magazine fiction.

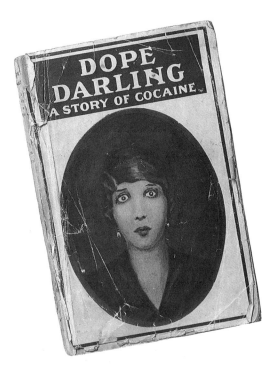

With his tongue firmly in his cheek, he compiled the dreadful drug-torn and cliché-crammed tale of *Dope Darling: A Story of Cocaine* under the pseudonym of 'Leda Burke'. This piece of jazz-age Jacqueline Susann proved to be everything he could have wished. *Dope Darling* not only found itself a publisher, but promptly sold out its full initial print run. Such an unlikely success, particularly from a follower of Bloomsbury, did not, however, set David off on a new and possibly lucrative career as a writer of sensational pulp fiction. Having served its purpose, *Dope Darling* was quickly forgotten as he put his energies into his struggling attempts to become a bookseller.

It was 1922 before the thirty-year-old, not-very-successful bookseller made his first substantial effort as a writer of fiction. He had already dipped into the world of the short story and three years earlier, with the help of E. M. Forster, had placed the story *The Old Dovecote* in the *English Review*, one of the many literary magazines of the time, but this time he made a more sustained stab at imaginative writing. Perhaps fairly, the inspiration came from a weekend break in the peaceful, literary haven of The Cearne, and was inspired by his newly pregnant wife.

One afternoon David and Ray were sitting in a field hoping to snatch a sight of some little fox cubs which he was certain were in the area. As time wore on, it seemed that their vigil was going to be disappointed, and David turned to his wife with the whimsical observation that he clearly was not going to see a fox that afternoon ... unless she should happen to turn into one suddenly. 'What would you do with me?' she asked in reply. It was a long time before her husband drew breath at the end of the tale which was his answer, and Ray was able to say to him, 'You must write that as a story.'

> I was a little surprised, as I had not been thinking of a story but only been occupied in teasing and making love to her by telling her how like she was to a wild animal, and how easily my intense love for her would overcome the trifling difficulties that would arise if she actually were transformed into one. I thought about the idea of a story all through tea and then wrote a synopsis based upon what I had been telling Ray, giving it the title of: *The Metamorphosis of Mrs Tebrick*.

In the days that followed, David sat at a slab of pine wood in the garden at The Cearne, slowly and carefully constructing the sentences which would build up into the strange tale of young Mrs Tebrick who one day, without any warning or explanation, turned suddenly into a fox, and of the dreadful trial that this metamorphosis, which took her each day further from human ways to those of an animal, placed on the devoted love of her husband. The result was a strangely effective and very individual novel, only ninety-one pages in length, relating the fantastical story of the feminine fox in a crisp, clear and oddly archaic language reminiscent of the writings of Daniel Defoe, and in a tone of deliberate and detailed matter-of-factness which had something of the flavour of an English Arabian Nights story. But the most remarkable and unusual thing was that, all the way through the book, there was the striking feeling that the author was not spinning a yarn, a fanciful fairy-tale, but describing the truth and actual fact. The dreadful dilemma of Mr Tebrick was a test of love that was intensely human. For *Lady Into Fox* was above all a love story.

The book was published by Chatto & Windus in November 1922 and was an instant and immense success. It left some traces of puzzlement in the minds of those critics who tried to categorize it, but its quality was firmly recognized by journalists and by his contemporaries.

> The story is not gloomy; it is sad and humorous. Freakish as it looks, it turns out to be a real morsel of art, conceived and written with a strange accomplishment. The vision, and the feeling under its control, give it life and a life of its own, for we cannot think of anything quite like it. Without confounding men and beasts – despite the metamorphosis – it knits them closer and brings us closer to them; and without description it brings a deep breath of the country.
>
> *Times Literary Supplement*

> The attempt to record, with every circumstance of matter-of-fact detail, a wholly impossible or 'momentous' event happening at the present time is a very difficult one. The sudden conversion of Mrs Tebrick into a vixen is, of course, in itself a wholly absurd fancy, and Mr Garnett does not try to give it plausibility by any optical illusion. But the extreme sobriety and exactness of his story does raise it out of the range of the absurd – we know it is outside the range of reality, yet we get seriously absorbed in the pathos of Mr Tebrick's life.
>
> *Times Literary Supplement*

> The most amazingly good story I have read for a long time ... I think it is perfectly done and could not have been done any other way. It is a quite fresh thing.
>
> H. G. Wells

David's unexpected book and its equally unexpected success produced pleased surprise both from his family and from his Bloomsbury friends. Time and again, when he had allowed himself to become miserable and frustrated over what he saw as his unproductive life, those friends had cheerfully reminded him of Sterne and his late and brilliant explosion upon the literary world with *Tristram Shandy*. If *Lady Into Fox* was not quite *Tristram Shandy*, it was nevertheless a work which combined quality and popular success in a way of which any author would have been proud and pleased. David was both, as well as

LADY INTO FOX

By

DAVID GARNETT

Illustrated with wood engravings by
R. A. GARNETT

LONDON
CHATTO & WINDUS
1922

relieved by the financial rewards of a literary success which, after years of struggling along on the meagre proceeds of the bookshop, came just at the right time to support Ray and their newly born son – named Richard after his grandfather – in a fashion to which they were beginning to think they would never have the chance to become accustomed.

David soon found that *Lady Into Fox* had propelled him into a position as a 'famous author'. His little book might not have the weight and importance of Virginia Woolf's works – *Jacob's Room* had appeared just before *Lady Into Fox* – or of Lytton Strachey's powerful *Eminent Victorians*, but no longer was he one of the agreeable nobodys loitering unproductively on the edges of Bloomsbury. He was a successful writer of some originality and style with a hit novel to his credit.

The accolades which came from the critics and the public for *Lady Into Fox* were soon followed by others from the literary world: the Hawthornden Prize of £100 for 'the greatest piece of imaginative literature published during the year' was presented to him by G. K. Chesterton and followed by another award, the even more lucrative James Tait Black Memorial Prize for fiction. Virginia Woolf wrote to him, 'At last, at last, the Hawthornden has chosen the right book. A thousand congratulations and please spend the £100 in writing another.' Chatto & Windus went through eight reprintings in just three years as the book was translated into more than a dozen foreign languages, and established itself as a tiny classic of English literature.

Having been catapulted into the public eye with his first real book, it now remained for David to confirm his new-found celebrity. Would he be one of those many writers who dazzle with just one splendid book before fizzling away into literary nothingness like a spent firework, or would he be able to sustain a career as an author and produce other works to equal *Lady Into Fox*? The answer was not long in coming.

In February 1924 Chatto & Windus published his second novel, *A Man in the Zoo*, and all the promises of *Lady Into Fox* were confirmed.

Once again, in a brief and pointed tale which mixed humans and animals – and David, half-scientist and half-hedonist, never forgot that man is himself but another species of animal – he had gathered an improbably curious series of events and related them in his cool, serious and neatly detailed style so that they became not only convincingly probable but highly effective.

The history of the foolishly passionate Mr Cromartie, shut up, at his own wish, in a cage between the orang outang and the chimpanzee in London Zoo in order to shock and spite the girl who would not yield to his proposals of love, was perhaps less fantastical than the tale of *Lady Into Fox* and it was told in a more modern style than the almost eighteenth-century language of its predecessor, but it showed all the individual flavour which had made the first book so effective.

A jacket woodcut by Ray Garnett

The Sailor's Return, the inspiration for the novel of the same name

Granted the fantasticality of his invention, Mr Garnett never strays very far from psychological realism in his working out of the consequences of [Mr Cromartie's actions]. The art of fiction is too frequently debased in practice by retaining the verisimilitude of the setting at whatever violence to the nature of human emotions. Only the finest artists can combine the two realities, and Mr Garnett follows at a distance the humbler tradition of *Zadig* and *Rasselas*, as opposed to that of *Tom Jones*. He has not been hustled into thinking that the intensity of emotion can be best expressed by passionate language ... [he] has discovered a vein of talent which gives much pleasure and is singularly his own.

Times Literary Supplement

The following year David scored again with *The Sailor's Return*, another tale mixing the commonplace and the fantastic, detailing the curious and sorry story of William Targett, the sailor who brings home to the little village of Maiden Newbarrow an African princess as his bride. This story, with its further echoes of Defoe, was greeted by the *Times Literary Supplement* as 'as teasing a performance as we have come to expect from him', a piece displaying the very personal and special style which the author had developed – a 'queer formalism' which 'for all its insistence on minute, fanciful detail has a certain grave and confiding warmth ... his beautifully precise writing cannot fail to attest his mastery of the psychological experience his narrative embraces'. Many rated it, and still rate it, as his best work.

Now thoroughly established as a considerable author, David was able to live in rather more comfort than before. He and Ray moved from London to the more expansive and relaxing atmosphere of Hilton Hall, set in the Cambridgeshire countryside near Huntingdon, although purposefully not – like The Cearne – at a foolishly romantic distance from civilization.

Hilton Hall, Hilton, Cambridgeshire

He sold his share in the bookselling business to a friend with more business aptitude that he had ever had, and settled down to the congenial life of being a full-time writer and an enthusiastically half-hearted country gentleman smallholder. He was based near enough to London to ensure that neither his social life, including his free-living extravagances among the Bloomsbury crowd, nor his extra-marital love life suffered. In 1927 his novel *Go She Must* appeared, followed the next year by a collection of short stories under the title of his earliest published piece, *The Old Dovecote*, and in 1929 by another novel *No Love*, like *Go She Must* an imaginative mixing and retelling of incidents from his own life.

During this time David had developed a fascination for aeroplanes and he had learned to fly, later becoming the owner of his own craft, a plywood machine which he piloted with a cavalier enthusiasm and perhaps not quite sufficient skill, but in which he found immense pleasure and the subject matter for some splendidly descriptive writing in the novel *The Grasshoppers Come* (1931) and his learning-to-fly notebooks *A Rabbit in the Air* (1932).

David Garnett at his
desk, Hilton, 1930

From the most modern aeroplanes to real, if dead, Indians
was quite a step, and the novel *Pocahontas* (1933) was by no
means the kind of work for which he had become best known.
Much more substantial than his early pieces – though with a
glimpse of *The Sailor's Return* in its subject matter – it was a full-
blown historical novel based on the much-used story of the adventurous John Smith and the famous Red Indian maiden who
saved his life. Written with his usual minute care for detail and
accuracy, it proved both popular and successful and David was
especially pleased, following some rather snooty anthropo-
logical questions from the other side of the Atlantic as to his
knowledge of Indian customs and lore, at its selection in America as a Book Society Choice. This was even more welcome as it
brought with it a large cheque, of which a part was immediately
earmarked for the purchase of his wooden aeroplane.

In the same year, rather to his surprise, he found himself
offered a regular job. It was not just any job, but the position of
Literary Editor on the *New Statesman*, and he accepted. It meant
more time in London, and less time for his own writing as he
devoted himself to organizing the literary content of the paper,
but he had not abandoned his novelist's career and in 1935 he
took a brief leave of absence from his new post to write *Beany-
Eye*, another novel compounded of remembered half-fact and
fiction, which took up and developed into a stunningly atmospheric short book a childhood memory of an episode concerning his father's brave efforts to tame a local workman who had
gone on the rampage around their home. In a book which
mixes, in a very televisual style, pictures of the British countryside, clearly described by a man who has an intimate practical
knowledge of its details, with a muscular narrative, he built up,
in his meticulous style, the powerful, unstable person of Joe
'Beany-Eye' Starling into a memorable character. In this way,
he produced a combination of the menacing and the matter-of-
fact which helped to make this disturbingly realistic piece even
more effective and moving than his earlier fantastical novels.

Beany-Eye was well received without winning the acclaim given to the earliest of his books. Perhaps David was now too familiar a presence in the book world to win rave reviews, but there is little doubt that, although it has been regularly reprinted in the half-century since its first appearance, this particular piece has never been valued at its real worth. At Edward's funeral, his sister Olive remarked that *Beany-Eye* would be the best memorial that her brother could have. For there was much of Edward in this story which illustrated the goodness and unthinking courage of a man who was able, through his humanity, to win the confidence of the simple but volatile labourer. But there was also much of David, of his writing talent in its most effective state. *Beany-Eye* might very well have been his best memorial as well.

When he got back to the *New Statesman*, David found that his job had gone. Righteous indignation won him handsome compensation and, in place of the editorial position which had gone beyond his reach, he was hired to write a regular column on Books in General. For the moment, at least, there were no more novels. David did not stop writing – far from it – but at this stage he put aside fiction and devoted himself to journalism and other areas of authorship and, finally, to his father's old position as a publisher's reader.

After the motorcycle death of T. E. Lawrence, he edited such of his old friend's letters and other writings as he could persuade their owners to bring forward, and later performed the same service for the stories of Henry James and the novels of Thomas Peacock, which had earlier been edited also by his grandfather, and he wrote introductions to editions of Voltaire and D. H. Lawrence. During the war years, part of which he spent attached to the Air Ministry and part as an active contributor to the psychological warfare department, he published several factual pieces, including 'a critical survey of the development of aerial warfare in all its branches, from the German conquest of Poland to the present day' and a children's book on the Battle of Britain. Later he began compiling the first of his three volumes of memoirs, which were to be published in the 1950s and 1960s, detailing – with as much frankness as was permissible in the moral climate of the time, and with a cheerfully casual reliance on his own not always accurate memory – those of his youthful experiences among the good, the great, the famous and the well-publicized which he felt like sharing with the world.

Ray's death from cancer in 1940 left him with two almost grown-up sons who soon had a stepmother only a little older than themselves when David surprised most of his friends by marrying Angelica Bell. In less than four years (thanks to the advent of twins) he was the father of four daughters and the harum-scarum life which they all lived at Hilton Hall, combined with his various activities in the literary world, filled everyone's days quite sufficiently to leave no place for imaginative writing.

John Nash, David Garnett, Vanessa Bell, Oliver Strachey, Dora Carrington, Duncan Grant and Barbara Bagenal go 'flying' (opposite top)

The real thing: David's plywood Klemm aeroplane (opposite bottom)

Angelica Garnett with her twin daughters, Frances and Nerissa

Twenty years had passed since the appearance of *Beany-Eye* when, in October 1955, David made a sudden and unheralded return to the world of fiction with a new novel from his old publishers, Chatto & Windus. This new work was one which was particularly close to its author's heart, for it dealt with the subject which had been, all his life, of such great importance to him. As with his first novel, the title said it all – *Aspects of Love*. It had not started out to be a novel. It had not started out, really, to be anything but a fragment of enjoyable writing. When David visited his son to read aloud – as he always liked to do – the little scene of love and passion that he had concocted around a French actress, a young English boy and a villa in France, that scene – that short story – was all that he had in mind. But the character of Rose, the actress, pleased him. Perhaps there was more in her than just this little episode. David went to work and, bit by bit, the original episode grew outer layers, extra incidents developed from it, and fresh characters came and went from the scene around the main protagonists of the story and their merry-go-round of amorous existence, and *Aspects of Love* grew into a full-scale book.

The slim volume of the completed novel was what one critic described as 'a hymn to Aphrodite, a garland of roses and myrtle'. The various progressions of the wickerwork of contrasting and intertwining love stories were described in a leisurely, unexaggerated style, reported with the same delicate narrative line that had characterized his earlier books, even if there was now a little more lushness, a little more self-indulgence in the telling. One unspectacular event in the unfolding years of his characters' lives followed another in the unhurried, unforced rhythm of real life, building to no speciously spaced climaxes or world-shattering events, but simply taking in the character and the various stages of the love affairs of the actress, Rose Vibert, of the youthful Alexis, and of his older and naturally libertine uncle, Sir George Dillingham, which make up the heart of the book.

First comes the passionate, reckless love of the teenage Alex for the older Rose, a love over-full of sentiment, driving him to ridiculous excesses in his boyish incomprehension that a woman could really care less for the hectic passion he offers than for the easy, undemanding love of an older man, a man of whom she can say only, 'He is kind, and for him loving means being kind.' Such extravagant sentimentalism fares badly in this tale – it is the sentimentalism of David's days before Bloomsbury and the 'enlightenment' he found there. He understands it and knows that neither man nor woman can live comfortably with it.

The love of Sir George is a less complicated and painful thing. It is a love that happily gives more than it demands, and it demands very little. It does not even demand fidelity. And neither does it offer it. It is the love which David calls the love of a libertine, and none the less genuine and sincere for, as his grandfather declared in so many of the aphorisms of *De Flagello*

David Garnett and
Quentin Bell, *c*.1940

Angelica Garnett,
artist

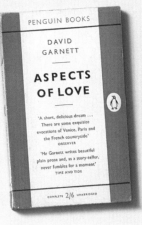

Myrteo, David and Sir George are both firm believers that lust without love is a poor thing.

> The torch of Cupid emits much heat but little light;
> but the torch of Eros enlightens even more than it inflames.
>
> *De Flagello Myrteo*, LXXIV

The love which they prize and practise unstintingly is no less a love than the more ardent and soul-stretching kind, it simply does not tie itself to the trappings and conventions laid on love by Church, society, state and romantic literature.

When George chooses Giulietta Trapani to pronounce his eulogy at the joyful wake he has willed instead of a gloomy funeral, he chooses knowingly, for Giulietta is his feminine counterpart; she too revels in the happy love of the libertine. Rose, on the other hand, has to be led to it. Her early days with George are full of happiness, but there is still too much of the old, unenlightened passion in her, and her jealous antics over his relationship with Giulietta make her as ridiculous as Alex has been over Rose herself, until Giulietta and George, in turn, succeed in bringing her round to their way of loving. And as the author passes in parade these two aspects of love, the soulful and the libertine, it is clear which of them he approves.

But these are not the only strands in this network of loving. Alex is not condemned as just a foolishly sentimental lover and George held up as a successful example of relaxed amorality. Into the story comes Jenny, the child of George and Rose's marriage. All three of the adults love Jenny but, as he grows older, George gradually discovers that his love for his daughter is the possessive, jealous love which he has always prided himself on never displaying with his mistresses. He allows his wife a lover, and even welcomes the young man into their home without the slightest animosity or envy, but he cannot bear to see the growing and awakening Jenny starting to move towards a life with another man. It is the last straw for him that the girl's new-found affections are turned towards the ever-present Alex. But Alex has come, through life, to a calmer state. He is able gently to turn aside the young girl's bursting first love and, leaving behind at the same time the memory of his own fateful early passion for Rose, he is rewarded by graduating, at last, to

libertinehood in the company of the splendid Giulietta. As for George, his fall from the amorous equilibrium in which he has led his life leads, quite simply, to the end of his life.

So how much of David himself is there in Alex and Sir George? Do we have here pictures of the young and sentimental David and the older and more morally comfortable David? Neither of the two characters, certainly, is a fully coloured self-portrait but, equally, the author has clearly invested each of his leading men with feelings and philosophies that were familiar to him. He knows his Rose and his Giulietta and he has known many of them. And what of the events of the story? The various relationships? It is tempting to see real-life parallels.

It is probably fallacious to see in the tale of Alex and Jenny the reflection of the tale of David himself and of Angelica, the beautiful young daughter of Duncan Grant and Vanessa Bell, although the pale shadow of revenge is hinted at in both relationships. In spite of his denials, does Alex, consciously or unconsciously, try to take Jenny from Sir George and from Rose in the way that George took Rose from him? And did David, who loved Vanessa and Duncan, perhaps woo Angelica from her unwilling parents partly for similar motives? Maybe. Maybe not. In the end, there is probably more of David and Angelica to be found in the feelings and moods depicted by George and Rose.

What is more likely is the reflection in the relationship between George and Jenny of that between David and his daughter, Amaryllis. It may or may not be evidence of this that the cover illustration on the original edition of *Aspects of Love* includes a portrait of Jenny, and its physical resemblance to the young Amaryllis is noticeable. It is always rather too easy to read significance into fiction, or to identify the author's friends and relations there, so perhaps it is safest simply to grant David the author's time-honoured right to take what he knows and has experienced and to build on it an imaginative fiction.

Although it was nominally set in the 1950s, the characters of *Aspects of Love* have a timeless quality and as they play out their story on a stage coloured by the vibrantly sun-stroked settings of Pau, of Rabelais's birthplace near Chinon, and of Venice, there is much less a feeling of 'now' than of 'whenever'. That 'whenever' which had been inhabited by David's beautiful people of the years between the wars, who had tried to live the morally relaxed and free life that Rose and Sir George and the lovely, uninhibited Giulietta enjoy in the pages of the novel, and which young Alex achieves in its final moments. That 'whenever' during which David himself discovered the comforts of being an uncomplicated libertine.

Here is *La Ronde* playing a different tune ... set in France and Italy and in the present day, [it] has no interest in contemporary problems or politics; it is, in essence, a pagan hymn written in praise of physical passion and the delights that go with it.

The Times

... a short, delicious dream in which there is not a plain girl or a corked bottle.

Observer

At a time when English novel-writing was embracing rougher and more raucous styles, the stylish, unaggressive and beautifully written *Aspects of Love* met with a fine critical response on both sides of the Atlantic, as its sales rocketed to such an extent that the first edition was completely sold out within a week of publication.

[David Garnett] has taken up where he left off, the same effortless charmer as before, the same evoker of reality which is somehow enchanted. There is only one touch of fantasy in *Aspects of Love*, but although the subject and the characters could not be more real and worldly, one senses that feet are rarely less than two inches off the ground and scenes are lit with an elfin glow ... Mr Garnett handles it all with an immense delicacy ... if we listen carefully, we will hear something of the truth about love. Perhaps one does – just a whisper.

The Sunday Times

The characters have blood in them, not mud, and passion, instead of a staled weariness. They behave sometimes unexpectedly – though not, on examination, improbably – but almost never meanly. And the style is a continuous delight, with a piquant limpidity which we have learned to expect from this author.

Daily Telegraph

Beautifully designed, compact and jewel-bright. This is a beautiful, passionate, exquisitely truthful novel. In a small compass Mr Garnett, with the utmost skill and economy, has enclosed a great deal of human life; I recognize and salute a quite unforgettable work of art.

Evening News

All the improprieties, the so-called Continental laxities which still send pleasant shivers down many an American spine, flower unblushingly ... David Garnett's flawless manner ... lifts *Aspects of Love* into the kind of fable told by Boccaccio and Balzac. You can safely place it somewhere near these masters on the same shelf.

New York Herald Tribune

High comedy in the grand manner, written with a pen dipped in champagne.

New York Times

David himself was pleased with his new novel. He wrote to his friend T. H. White, the wayward author of *The Once and Future King*:

I have recently written my best book – a short novel ... called *Aspects of Love*. It was a wonderful feeling to be writing seriously again: – and writing very differently. It is a good deal in conversation & it is incredibly economical – in fact too concentrated I fear for most readers – not ten lines of padding or repetition in the book. The effect – (on those on whom it has an effect) is like a very dramatic short play.

Not everyone agreed with him, of course, and with his friend, the novelist Sylvia Townsend Warner, who wrote to him crowing delightedly:

> What a pleasure it is to see real writing again, and real construction and pleasure in life! It was like coming to a perfectly cooked chicken again after sitting at endless tables of Birdseye and bad cocktails.

There were those who would not be seduced by a book which had neither a meaningful message to impart nor a purposefully thundering action, those who denied the usefulness of storytelling unless that story had a purpose. They had no time for the brand of writer which David admired and strove to emulate, a brand which he described, years later, in a 'Confession of Faith', prefacing his last book of memoirs:

> There have always been a few rare individuals, artists who are not concerned with preaching, or seeking a revenge upon the littleness of life, but who have accepted it, have held it up in their stories. Such writers are regarded as immoralists and as escapists by the propagandists and preachers. But in my opinion these pure artists are our best guides.

Also, even in 1955, not everyone found David's championing of the lazily libertine moral standards of his characters acceptable. Even White grudgingly, but sincerely, voiced his disapproval:

> I can't help it – I believe that people ought to be monogamous . . . that if they consciously take a solemn vow in public they should stick to it – or not take it – and that women ought not to behave like headstrong babies . . . I hate Rose . . . for going to bed with Alexis first, then tossing him over for Sir George, and then taking him and other lovers. Surely women are dependable people as well as men? . . . I think your Rose is a selfish, short-sighted self-admirer and a bore . . . The only sensible person in your book was Jenny – who really meant what she said – and Alexis ought to have married her – I repeat 'married' – and he should have been faithful to her as she to him.

But David was quick to answer him back, expressing equally strong feelings:

> Your letter reveals a mediaeval monkish attitude. I, as I think you know, believe in love and the tenderness and understanding which reciprocated happy love brings with it. I believe that the sexual instinct in normal people is good: possibly the highest good. You can find out what I think about fidelity in several of my books. It is a large part of the subject of *Lady Into Fox* and of *The Sailor's Return*. The exclusiveness of love and its secret private nature is the underlying subject of *A Man in the Zoo*. My experience is that an exclusive passion as a first love is extremely unusual: most young people are more likely to mate well if they experiment a good deal . . . Rose is in my opinion a healthy, normal and delightful woman. She is exceptionally sincere and trustful and follows her excellent instincts.

What he did not suggest to his friend in defence of his book and his characters was that White compare his own desperately unhappy personal and sexual life, led under the moral code by which he judged so fiercely, with David's own rather friendly succession of pleasant and pleasing mistresses.

The success of *Aspects of Love* led David to remain in the realm of fiction and, in the years that followed, he added regularly to his stock of novels with *A Shot in the Dark* (1958), *A Net for Venus* (1959), *Two by Two* (1963), *Ulterior Motives* (1966), *A Clean Slate* (1971), *The Sons of the Falcon* (1972), a blood and thunderous tale of historical Armenia based on a story told to him by a Russian exile, *Plough over Bones* (1973), in which he used memories gathered during his time with the Quaker relief services in the First World War, the short stories *Purl and Plain* (1973) and *Up She Rises* (1977). He did not abandon his editorial work and, among other pieces, published his fascinating correspondence with T. H. White and the writings and letters of another friend of Bloomsbury, the strange and ill-fated Dora Carrington. He also continued his memoirs and, although the promised fourth volume did not appear, at the age of ninety he published a last volume, reminiscing over the *Great Friends* of his childhood and youth. If he had begun his career as a writer rather later than he might have, he certainly made up for those early lost years in his later life.

In 1970 he moved to live in the French countryside and he stayed there, comfortably writing and indulging in his last great love affair – with French cooking – until his death, eleven years later. Since his earliest visits there, as a child, he had always been fond of France, and its temperament, its people and its food suited him. It is a country which, to the English, has always represented, truly or mythically, the kind of sexual and moral standards and behaviour in which David so actively believed. But, as David and all those who actually get further than the flimsy fleshpots of weekend Paris soon discover, it is more than that. France is a whole mentality, with as strict a morality as Britain. It is just a different morality.

It was no hazard that the action of *Aspects of Love* had been placed in France and that Sir George Dillingham, who shared and shares David's philosophies and predilections, chose to spend the best years of his life there, on the very hill where Rabelais had lived. As David's daughter, Henrietta, confirmed in later years, her father did not precisely draw a picture of himself in Sir George, but having created Sir George he did begin to behave like him in some ways. It was not such a bad model, and even if there were no flaming wake at his passing, he lived up cheerfully and unpretentiously to his lines in *Aspects of Love*: '*Pone merum et talos. Pereat qui crastina curat*', or 'for those who are without Latin':

> Set down the wine and the dice
> And perish the thought of tomorrow.

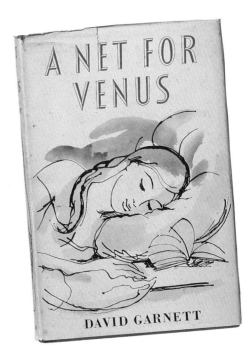

A jacket illustration by Angelica Garnett

David Garnett at home, 1972

Garnett on Stage and Screen

David Garnett never wrote a piece for the stage or for the screen that was actually produced. Not unless you count a handful of cheerfully amateurish concoctions designed for family and friends to perform. In spite of numerous attempts at plays, and a screenplay, *Seek No Further*, adapted from an unpublished novel, which almost made it to the screen under the Korda regime, his contribution to the fiction of the nation remained in the form of novels, and novels only. Although he was extremely happy that other people should remake and remould his works for different media if they so wished, he never attempted to adapt any of his published novels himself.

From the moment of his very first success with *Lady Into Fox*, his works awakened interest among both theatre and film folk, and Garnett happily sold the rights to transfer a good number of his earliest novels to stage and screen, sometimes on more than one occasion. Predictably, *Lady Into Fox* attracted numerous bids of all kinds and *A Man in the Zoo* aroused the interest of no less a star than Charlie Chaplin, who fancied himself in the role of the novel's caged hero. Unfortunately, most of the enthusiastic producers who contributed in this way to the Garnett family coffers ended up with nothing to show for their money. Having secured the rights, they became slowly and painfully aware that, even given that they might be able to lift the special flavour of Garnett's work off the printed page, his plots and characters left them with some insuperable practical problems.

How, for example, were they to cope on stage with the transformation of Mrs Tebrick from lady into fox? And, even if this were more feasible on film, having replaced the leading lady with a nice little vixen early in the first reel, how, without an incredible feat of animal training, or the *Roger Rabbit* animation techniques of later days, were they to make the wretched animal act? How did one make a fox play cards, appreciate stereopticon pictures of Spain, or feign dead on cue? Australian Joanne Lane got closest to this when she succeeded in training a whole team of foxes to perform one of the necessary actions apiece, but having got this far, she was unable to get the film off the ground.

A Man in the Zoo had equally daunting drawbacks. Here the star of the show had to play opposite a belligerent orang outang and a chimpanzee. Even for Chaplin that was a challenge, one at which he jibbed and which was only taken up in later years in a short-lived British television production.

Lady Into Fox did, on the other hand, make its way on to the stage, and it did so in what, when you think about it, was the logical way to present the tightly worded episodes of Garnett's highly fantastical tale in a living performance. It was played with no words at all. Just movement. Quite who first thought of making a ballet out of *Lady Into Fox* is obscured by the years, but it seems that around 1937 the choreographer Antony Tudor had got far enough in his plans to use Garnett's story as the basis for a revue ballet scena, starring Ballet Rambert ballerina Maude Lloyd, to have selected a musical score from the works of the French composer Arthur Honegger and to have had scenic and costume designs made by Sophie Fedorovitch. Tudor's version did not come to pass, but the idea had taken root and, two years later, the Ballet Rambert staged the first theatrical production of a Garnett novel with their dance version of *Lady Into Fox* devised and created by the young choreographer and dancer, Andrée Howard.

Of necessity, Miss Howard simplified and shortened the storyline of the novel, eliminating the book's later scenes which, with Silvia Tebrick become wholly and horrifyingly a fox, focus on the dilemma of her desperate husband. In this version it was Silvia – woman, fox and prima ballerina – who was the central character, and the ballet ended with her flight to freedom from civilization, rather than with Mr Tebrick's search for his wife and her dreadful fate at the fangs of the local foxhounds.

Following Tudor's plan, the music was taken from the works of Honegger – oddly, not from his dramatic works, but from a group of his keyboard pieces – and arranged by Charles Lynch; and in place of Miss Fedorovitch, the sets and costumes were entrusted to another Russian ballet designer, Nadia Benois, niece of the famous French designer of the Diaghilev company, Alexandre Benois. Miss Howard, who had intended to dance the star role of Silvia herself, was prevented from doing so by an injury, and when Celia Franca, who had been selected to replace her, also fell victim to injury in rehearsal, the role was filled by seventeen-year-old Sally Gilmour, taking a lead role for the first time in her career.

The first performance of *Lady Into Fox* was given on 15 May 1939 at the tiny Mercury Theatre, the London base of the Rambert company, and it met with an overwhelming theatrical and critical response. The *Daily Telegraph* hailed 'a masterpiece', the *Dancing Times* referred to the 'inspired choreography' of the vixen's role, and the principal papers were in accord in praising the combination of talents which had produced this outstanding dance-drama. Miss Howard, whose great talent lay in creating dramatic, small-scale dance pieces built around a tight group of strongly drawn characters, and in using as much mime

Rambert Dance Company: *Lady into Fox* (1939) with Sally Gilmour and Charles Boyd as Mr and Mrs Tebrick (right)

as regular dance steps in her choreography, had told Garnett's story extremely effectively. In the process she invented a dazzling central role for the dancer cast as the fox, and Sally Gilmour profited from the opportunity and gave a star performance which launched her on a prima ballerina's career. The Honegger score was praised everywhere as adding to the effectiveness of the piece, and Mlle Benois's three sets – and, in particular, her costume for the star dancer, in which the bustle of the Victorian lady's dress became the tail of the fox – won regular plaudits:

> The dress of the fox is very skilfully done. She wears fox-red tights, with black hands and feet, a russet-red close-fitting bodice and a brush of the same colour, made of soft flounces, tipped with white. A red wig and slanting eyes complete her foxy appearance.

> *Daily Telegraph*

Garnett was delighted with the ballet and, in particular, with Miss Gilmour, and he was by no means alone. Such was the success of the first production of *Lady Into Fox* that the company was obliged to play it every night of their London season and, when even that did not prove sufficient to satisfy the demand for seats, they returned a few weeks later, after their previously scheduled Birmingham dates, for an additional three-week season at the Mercury Theatre, with the new ballet featuring in every night's entertainment.

Rambert Dance Company: *Lady into Fox* (1939) with Sally Gilmour and Walter Gore as Mr and Mrs Tebrick

Lady Into Fox remained in the Ballet Rambert's repertoire for more than a decade. It was played throughout Britain and in the company's overseas performances in Australia, New Zealand, Germany and France, often on much larger stages than the pocket-handkerchief platform for which it had been invented. It was also mounted at New York's Center Theatre, in 1940, by the American Ballet Theatre, in a production in which Andrée Howard finally got to play the role she had conceived.

Rambert Dance Company: *The Sailor's Return* (1947) with Stanley Newby (The Revd Cronk) and Sally Gilmour (Tulip)

Eight years and a number of successful dance works later, Miss Howard took a second dip into the Garnett *opus* when she wrote, choreographed and designed a ballet version of *The Sailor's Return* for the Rambert company. This was an even more adventurous step than *Lady Into Fox* had been, for not only was it a two-act ballet (as opposed to the three scenes in one act of the earlier piece) but it was set to a specially commissioned score by the company's musical director, Arthur Oldham, the first time such a sizeable commission had been issued in the British ballet world.

The result was, once again, an unequivocal success. As in the earlier ballet, Miss Howard had tactfully thinned and re-shaped (although this time not truncated) Garnett's tale to take the main emphasis away from the male protagonist – here the sailor of the title – and place it firmly and effectively on the prima ballerina role, the black African princess doomed to widowhood and drudgery by the suspicious hatred of the people of her husband's Dorset home town. Sally Gilmour starred again, deeply dyed as the tragic Tulip, and the pre-mière, on 2 June 1947 at Sadler's Wells Theatre, was greeted with great enthusiasm. The *New Statesman* spoke of 'a remark-

Rambert Dance
Company: *The
Sailor's Return* (1947)
with Sally Gilmour
as Tulip

able achievement', Caryl Brahms in the *Evening Standard*
praised 'a great advance on anything Miss Howard has yet
created ... simple and sensitive ... a performance of integrity
and distinction', while *The Times* waxed very fulsome indeed:

> Miss Andrée Howard showed in *The Mermaid* and *Lady Into Fox*
> that she is an artist of the theatre (choreographer and designer)
> who can from a quick and keen imagination produce a master-
> piece. To these two small works, each in its proper size a master-
> piece, she has now added a third of somewhat greater size and
> emotional range ... *The Sailor's Return* ... is a ballet that has
> dramatic action and inevitability, whose truth has been im-
> aginatively converted into the language of dancing, and because
> it is true to life is also beautiful.

Arthur Oldham's vigorously dramatic score raised an eye-
brow or two among those used to more sophisticated ballet
music, but it proved extremely effective and allowed Miss
Howard to stage several outstanding solo set pieces, notably a
marvellously uninhibited dance for Tulip, and several stand-
out character numbers, including one for the very young John

Gilpin in the incidental role of the rabbit-catcher. The *Dancing Times* described the piece as 'her most ambitious work so far', before going on:

> This is a most interesting work which will enhance Andrée Howard's reputation as a choreographer. That she should choose so exacting an author as David Garnett and successfully adapt his work into dance forms proves that she is at her best when faced with exact and actual problems laid down by a literary work.

Those problems were rather more real to the men of the film world. One by one, Garnett's works were taken up by the celluloid Caesars and, one by one, they were dropped. *Lady Into Fox* went through the whole business of options, plans, more plans and no tangible results several times; Chaplin failed to come up trumps on *A Man in the Zoo*; and, when Garnett chose to sell the film rights of *Pocahontas* to Charles Laughton, who had a yen to appear as John Smith, rather than to film baron Alexander Korda, he found that Laughton was caught up unendingly in work for Korda which prevented him from taking the project further. The word 'film' became something like a recurring mirage to Garnett. It was one thing selling film rights to his novels; quite another to see those films ever made. Until the very latest years of his life, he had to be content with just one filmed version of his work – and that was a very curious one indeed.

In the summer of 1935 Cecil Beaton decided he was going to make a film. Not a professional affair with real actors, of course, for this was 1935 and the young Beaton was not yet the celebrity he later became but merely one of the classily connected young folk who spent their weekends socializing among the tennis courts and champagne bottles at Britain's prettier country houses. This particular weekend the activity for the guests at Ashcombe was not tennis, but a film. They would all be actors.

It was done properly. A professional director and cameraman were brought down from London and a regular scenario was prepared, based on Garnett's *The Sailor's Return*. When Beaton approached Garnett for his permission, the author wryly warned him that something would surely go wrong. So many attempts to put the piece on film had already been hamstrung by one situation or another that there was clearly a jinx on it. If the young man wished to continue with his project, that was fine by Garnett, but he warned him that, if nothing else, it would surely pour with rain all weekend.

But it did not. There were plenty of incidents, but it did not rain. The make-up man turned out to be rather less of an expert than he had claimed to be, and Lady Caroline Paget, an aspiring actress cast as Tulip, who had to endure being painted chocolate, or at least coffee-brown, for her role, faced the prospect of undergoing running repairs between every shot as she

'Let's make a film . . .', Ashcombe, 1935

smudged her way through the script, until the latest products of Mr Max Factor, hurriedly ordered from London, arrived on the set. Then the black child (a veteran of the film *Sanders of the River*) hired to play Tulip's baby failed to turn up on time, and a search party had to go out to scour the railways and roads of the county in search of this all-important cast member, while the gardener's daughter was put on stand-by as an emergency understudy. Props, as ever, took on a life of their own, and a heavily laden cart driven by the hero and heroine disintegrated seconds after it had rumbled awkwardly out of camera shot. But the amateur actors, headed by Lady Caroline, with Beaton himself as the sailor Targett, the future Poet Laureate John Betjeman (then the *Evening Standard* film critic) as the interfering clergyman, and John Sutro, a director of London Films but an amateur actor, in the villain's role, and supported by such of the local folk as could be persuaded to take part, had a splendid time. The result was a little film which, if it still exists, would be a splendid collector's prize, and a hole of 300 bottles in Ashcombe's wine cellars.

Attempts to make a more significant film version of *The Sailor's Return* continued over the following decades. The Austrian film director Berthold Viertel tried for a number of years to get a production off the ground, before Hollywood's William Wyler, then at the height of his fame, took up the rights and, in turn, attempted vainly to raise interest and finance for the film among the American studios. He, in the end, had no more luck than Viertel, as a likely source of finance vanished at an advanced stage of negotiations when a horrified filmocrat realized that the female star of the show was a deeply unbankable black. It was not until forty-five years after Beaton's amateur mini-film that *The Sailor's Return* finally got a rather more substantial film treatment.

The theme of racial intolerance involved in the novel's story of tragic fidelity, and its featuring of a black leading lady, large among the elements which had previously hindered the planning and financing of a production, had by now become not only acceptable but fashionable. However, it still took producer Otto Plaschkes and director Jack Gold, who picked up the film rights in 1970, seven years of effort before they succeeded in getting together a package which would allow them to go into production.

Early in the struggle, the National Film Finance Corporation responded positively to the eager pair but, even with that lump of monetary backing secured, they still had enormous difficulty in finding a production house with time and money to invest in their project. Finally it happened. The newly formed film branch of Thames Television, Euston Films, had made a very successful start as a production house with its highly profitable television film series *The Sweeney*, Gold had scored a hit with the Quentin Crisp film *The Naked Civil Servant*, and Jeremy Isaacs, Thames's programme controller, had already shown interest in a possible collaboration with Plaschkes in the wake

Actors and actresses for a weekend: Cecil Beaton, Lady Caroline Paget, and one little professional

Ariel Productions: *The Sailor's Return* (1978) with Tom Bell (William Targett) and Shope Shodeinde (Tulip)

of his success with the film *Georgy Girl*. They all came together, Euston Films took on *The Sailor's Return* and, late in 1977, the first professional film of a Garnett work went into production.

Playwright and scriptwriter James Saunders, the author of *Next Time I'll Sing to You*, translated the novel into a screenplay, Tom Bell was cast as the sailor opposite Nigerian actress Shope Shodeinde as his persecuted bride, and the two-hour film was shot in the Cotswolds – an area more easily redecorated as part of mid-Victorian England than the original Dorsetshire setting of the novel. It was released the following year, taking pride of place as the gala finale of the London Film Festival, and met with a mixed reaction. The *Sunday Express*'s Richard Barkley acclaimed it as 'a film of rare quality' which 'provides a profoundly moving experience ... one of the most heart-rending films I have seen this year', but others were less impressed and the movie was not picked up for general release. Instead it was shown to a wider public on Thames Television in 1980. Its racial content was advertised and emphasized over and above everything else and, as a result, the film was awarded a share in the Martin Luther King Prize for 1980 as one of the year's works most reflecting the late Dr King's ideals in Britain, but still it did not find itself a place in the cinema.

Ariel Productions:
The Sailor's Return
(1978), Tom Bell
and Shope
Shodeinde

In spite of an endless succession of 'maybe's and 'almost's, Garnett's contribution to the stage and screen in more than half a century up to the end of the 1970s was limited to the one film, one television play and two ballets. Small wonder, then, that the ageing author took a ruefully disbelieving attitude whenever approached over a new version of one of his works and, pleasing though the idea of a musical play – particularly one with a score by the newly celebrated composer of *Jesus Christ Superstar* – based on his *Aspects of Love* might have been, he was scarcely counting on its ever coming to the stage.

Aspects of Love had already attracted the attention of the French film-maker Jean Renoir, who had proposed a cinema version with Jeanne Moreau starring in the role of Rose, but that project had gone the way of so many others like it – why should this one by any different? But Garnett was counting without Lloyd Webber's tenacity and his unshakeable admiration for *Aspects of Love*. The musical stage version of the novel would take even longer to come to fruition than the film of *The Sailor's Return* had done and David Garnett, sadly, would not be around to see Rose, George, Alexis and Giulietta Trapani brought so vividly to life on stage, but the year of 1989 at last completed the author's hat-trick. With the opening of *Aspects of Love* at the Prince of Wales Theatre, London, the novelist who wrote only for the printed page had been presented not only both on stage and screen, but in straight drama, in dance and in the many-faceted terms of the modern musical theatre.

Pau and the Pyrenees

When David Garnett chose the southern French town of Pau as the home-away-from-home of Sir George Dillingham, the central character of his novel, *Aspects of Love*, it was not such an exotic choice as it might seem. In Garnett's lifetime, Pau was quite simply the most British of all French towns. This lovely, but apparently unremarkable, Béarnais market town, perched on a strange cliff above a river born of the snows of the Pyrenean mountain range, and expanded from a hamlet into a royal residence 600 years ago 'because of the beauty of its site and the good hunting in the region', had become such a favourite with British expatriates that it had taken on all the appearance of an unofficial outpost of the Empire, and it was with good reason that it was cheerfully known by the French as *la ville Anglaise*.

Nowadays, things are rather different. The Pau of today is a dynamic and thriving French provincial town which no longer centres its daily life either on its market or on servicing the British tourist. It has also come a long way from being a hamlet. Nearly 90,000 people live in this, the capital city of the beautiful Béarn region, a total which rises to 150,000 when the surrounding *agglomération* of suburbs is taken into consideration.

In the past forty years, while many other similar provincial areas have watched their inhabitants increasingly move away towards the big cities, Pau – which even at the height of its anglicized fame in earlier days stayed resolutely pint-sized – has grown to double its former population. The source of the town's enormous increase in importance can be resumed in one word – gas. Since the discovery of oil and natural gas in the area some forty years ago, Pau has found itself a new vocation as a city of science and technology and, far from losing its population to the metropolis, it has steadily attracted new blood to the Béarn as it has regularly grown and prospered.

This growth, and the stream of inhabitants which the new industrial and commercial activities brought to a town whose main asset had, for more than a century, been its natural climate and setting, set in motion considerable change. And it was a change which moved much more speedily than things have a habit of doing in this most staunchly yeoman of regions. The buildings of industry, commerce and scientific research and of their employees, great and humble, rose up swiftly to join – and

43

Pau, ancient and modern: Place Georges
Clemenceau, 1989

in some cases replace – the serried rows of grand villas built by
well-off folk in the days when Pau was internationally famed as
a health and holiday resort.

The great parks and gardens surrounding the bigger mansions were subdivided to build houses of dimensions more practical for the middle years of the twentieth century, and some of
the finest houses fell under the developers' demolition ball.
Nowadays, in the outlying districts, the big, old L-shaped Béarnais farmhouses with their vast iron gates rub shoulders with
manufacturing and commercial buildings, and in the town's
central Place Georges Clemenceau a great glass Nouvelles Gal-
eries chain store towers alongside a turreted building of the previous century.

Like a healthy patient, Pau has taken all these grafts on to
its ancient heart strongly and happily. The presence of so many
great gardens in what was formerly the outer part of the town
has meant that the modern Pau has many more green areas and
great trees in its residential areas than most other cities and, in
some places, the speed of development has left little pockets of
smallholdings in what have become city areas, where a pig and
a cow or two lounge unconcernedly on the grass on the plot next
to a 1980s' construction. But, apart from a few inevitable archi-
tectural disasters, such as the extension of the seventeenth-
century Lycée Louis-Barthou with a concrete 1960s' block, or
the implantation of apartment buildings from the same period
alongside the grandiose villas and hotels on the great Boulevard des Pyrénées, old and new cohabit very well in Pau.

For the coming of so much that is new to the town and to its
surrounding countryside has in no significant way wiped away
the old. Pau is a very venerable town, and the imprint and
legacy of its two periods of worldwide fame and greatness are
extremely visible today.

The first memorable event in Pau's existence, the one
which really launched it internationally, took place in the six-
teenth century. It was then that this little town of something
like a thousand souls provided France with a king, and a good
king at that. Although other sons of the city – from Napoleon's
General Bernadotte, the ancestor of the present Swedish royal
family, to Dumas's musketeer Porthos – have made a name for
themselves over the years, the Palois have always rejoiced
above all in *lou nouste Henric* ... 'Our Henry'. More than 400
years after his reign, Our Henry is still by far the most important personality in the town. His name has been attached to
local brands of cheese and chocolate, his face pops up everywhere, even iced on the top of a chocolate cake in a *pâtisserie*
window, the supplier of grave ornaments at the cemetery gates
calls his shop 'Lou Nouste Henric', and whenever you spot a
period picture or a statue, there is decidedly more than a
fifty–fifty chance that the subject will turn out to be Henry.

In the reign of Louis XIV, when it was decreed that the
cities of France should erect both a statue of their monarch and
a church in their main squares as a daily reminder of the pres-

Lou Nouste Henric: King Henry of France
and Navarre

PAU *Ville authentique*

ence and power of Church and State in their lives, independently minded Pau managed to fudge its contribution. When the church finally got off the drawing board, it progressed so slowly that it was never finished, and the foundations finally became those of the town's theatre. Although the Palois did put up the obligatory statue, it was a very small statue, and the inscription on it did not actually mention the king by name, simply calling him 'the grandson of *lou nouste Henric*'. It was later replaced by a different, bigger statue – of Henry, of course. And that one, like the theatre, is still there.

Henry was born at the Château of Pau, now a towering jigsaw of an edifice added to and re-made through the years, which stands at the heart of the old town, on the long cliff-face above the banks of the Gave de Pau and the ancient Pont de Jurançon, and which had been for several centuries one of the homes of the royal family of Navarre. He was born a Protestant, for his grandmother, Marguerite d'Angoulême, had welcomed clerics from the Lutheran school and even the great Calvin himself to her court, and Henry's mother, the zealous Queen Jeanne, had sent her country bloodily into battle against Catholic France on behalf of the Protestant cause.

Henry, cannily married to the daughter of the powerful and Catholic Catherine de Medici, was as King of France to be instrumental in ending the religious wars in his country for

Pau, Rue de la
Préfecture, *c*.1900

many years and, by the Edict of Nantes, in establishing religious tolerance in France for the twenty years of his reign. Both a good and popular king, he was indeed a native son to be proud of, and even though he never returned to Pau after embracing the crown of France and an expedient Catholicism, he was always attached enough to his birthplace to call himself 'King of France and Navarre' and to claim that he had given France to Béarn rather than the other way round. At least, that was the way the tale was told in Pau.

After Henry's death, the Bourbon dynasty which he had instituted continued through the eight monarchies up to the Revolution, while Pau – since 1620 officially a part of France – continued its untroubled, rural existence as a medium-sized market town and the capital of the Navarre region. It grew a bit from time to time, but changed little as life in the Béarn moved on at its usual unhurried pace for something like two centuries. It was then that the British arrived and brought with them Pau's second period of notoriety.

The first British folk to become particularly aware of Pau were soldiers. On the way home from the victorious campaign against Napoleon in 1814, the Duke of Wellington's men were surprised and delighted to find themselves greeted with flowers and enthusiasm by the citizens of the charming Béarnais capital. It was a reception some of them remembered fondly, and a number of veterans later returned to the region where, with their demob pay, they settled down in the friendly farmlands surrounding the town. Some of their officers came back, too, to spend holidays with their families in the warm, relaxing atmosphere of Pau itself. As word of mouth slowly spread the news of the town's healthy attractions among the British upper-middle classes, Pau began to attract a regular, if not yet over-large, British contingent, fleeing from the winter months at home to a more agreeable climate.

In 1819 the town welcomed its most distinguished Anglo-Saxon visitor to date when Thomas Douglas, 5th Earl of Selkirk, the celebrated colonizer of Canada, took up residence. Dying of lung disease, he found relief in the still, sedative air of Pau and, at the same time, focused the attention of some members of British society on the place he had accidentally selected as his refuge. A few years later the town again made the news when the famous poet, Alfred de Vigny, met and married the daughter of a British holidaymaker there. Little by little Pau was creeping out of anonymity and, little by little, it was evoking interest among the British.

That interest was further aroused by one Mrs Ellis, a lady of letters and the wife of a respected missionary, who published in 1834 a book called *Summer and Winter in the Pyrénées*, illustrated with effective, romantic pictures of the area drawn by her own very adept hand. Mrs Ellis was not satisfied with the public hygiene of Pau and was quite scandalized at the local people's lack of knowledge of how to serve tea properly, but she found the town extremely attractive, both in its climate and its natural beauty, and communicated her enthusiasm in her writing.

The real vogue for Pau, however, was started a few years later. The moving force was a Scotsman, Dr Alexander Taylor. Having himself come to Pau in 1838 for the benefit of his health after an exhausting period spent as an army doctor in Spain, Taylor took up residence in the town and, in 1843, published an enthusiastic book on his adopted home. *De l'Influence Curative du Climat de Pau et des Eaux Minérales des Pyrénées sur les Maladies*,

Stone walls and L-shaped farmhouse, *c*.1950

Pau: the Pont de Jurançon, the Château (centre) and on the right the Hôtel Gassion

with its fervent claims for the efficacy of Pau's 'greenhouse' weather and the local waters as a cure for tuberculosis and respiratory diseases, the two most prevalent ailments of the age, was a perfectly splendid piece of tourist propaganda. Taylor treated his subject with colourful conviction, backed up his claims with some reasonably solid pseudo-scientific data, which surprisingly few would challenge, and wrote in an attractive and credible style.

The fashion for *climatisme* – the use of different climactic conditions and natural waters as therapy for a multitude of illnesses – was just getting under way and *The Climate of Pau* hit an eager and inquisitive public at just the right moment. In the same way that, in modern times, the latest diet fad is snapped up by those who have failed with all the earlier ones, the book sold well and Pau became an increasingly popular health resort. Since there was sufficient truth in Taylor's book, many of those who came to Pau and who benefited from spending their winter months in its warm, moist and almost wholly windless climate, became regular visitors or even residents. And as the years passed, they were followed, in turn, by friends who had no need of a cure, but who came for the agreeable atmosphere and the growing social life they might encounter. As the British presence in the town grew and grew, so Pau began to turn itself into a little Britain in which the newcomers might live, in the style to which they were accustomed at home, in the midst of south-west France.

All around the old town of Pau new villas sprang up, homes built in the grand British country-house style of the period, set among grounds filled with flowers and, above all, with trees. The local shops began to stock the necessities of British life – British fabrics for the ladies' dresses, British tea, coal from Scotland – and gradually a whole set of specifically British shops and institutions moved in. Often these were run by intrepid expatriates, such as the vicar's wife, Mrs Hattersley, who set up the Pension Hattersley in competition with a French *pension* which called itself, hopefully, *un Boarding-House*.

There were British banks, a British school and, given the number of invalids in town, John Jarvis's English pharmacy was a particularly popular institution. By the time a decade or two had passed he had competition from 'The London Pharmacy' and a whole selection of other similar establishments. Another bold Briton, a tailor who set up as 'Old England' on the corner of the main square, little realized that he was starting what would one day become a chain of shops.

The British abroad not only required their home comforts but also their home entertainments and, one by one, British field sports were transplanted on to the plains of the Béarn. Outside the town, to the north, a steeplechasing track was erected, and 1842 saw the inauguration of the Pau hunt. Horses, hounds, carriages, pink coats and a liberal supply of French foxes galloped across the lands to the north and east of the town, which was divided up into the Home Circuit, the Hill

'Pau Golf Club and the Pyrenees,' 1893, by
Allen C. Sealy

District, Old England and Haut and Bas Leicestershire for
the enjoyment of those who missed the hunts of the real
Leicestershire.

In 1856 four Scotsmen – Colonel Hutchinson, Colonel
Anstruther, Major Pontifex and the Archdeacon Sapte – pur-
chased a large piece of land to the other side of town, and there
they laid down the first nine holes of the Pau Golf Club. It was
the first golf course to be built on the Continent and, apparently, one of the first anywhere to admit lady players. The following year the Duke of Hamilton came to play there and
presented a medal, which is still played for to this day.

Like the race course and so much else of what the British
brought to the area, the Pau Golf Club is still very much in evidence. Its elegant, old clubhouse stands at the top of eighteen
immaculate holes, the green, green grass of the course mani-
cured to perfection in a fashion more English than English. The
walls of the building are covered with the traditional black
honours boards, on which the names of club secretaries are
gilded alongside the often titled or military winners of the
McNab Cup, the McDona Cup, the Kilmaire Cup and the
Brooke Cup. In the bridge room can be seen the remnants of the
old library – leatherbound volumes of *The Queen* and *Lady's
Newspaper*, *Harper's Magazine* of 1886, the novels of Walter
Besant and Marie Corelli, a large illustrated volume on 'The
Anatomy of the Horse', and aged photographs of past players,
one group including the fat form of socialite Eustace 'Scroby'
Ponsonby, the author of some of the worst lyrics to have graced
the West End musical stage.

The English Club or *Cercle Anglais*, another old-established institution, which originally had its home on the town's main square, later shifted its headquarters to the gilded salons of the glorious new Hôtel Gassion, the most splendid of Pau's latter-day establishments. The Gassion is no longer a hotel, for the pre-war days in which such luxurious establishments flourished have gone, but among the apartments into which its rooms have been divided, the *Cercle Anglais* still remains in its old place.

There is no longer a British consul in Pau, and the churches – the Anglican St Andrews, Christ Church and the Presbyterian kirk – have nowadays given way to a shared Protestant vicar who includes Pau on his circuit. But everywhere the names of the nineteenth-century British and American families who peopled the town, and the names of their fondly remembered home towns, can be seen in the street names and on the gateposts of the vast estates which were once their properties – Rue Buckingham; the Villa Ridgway; the Clinique Maryland, once the home of the novelist Dornford Yates; the Villa St Helens, now the quarters of the local *préfet*; the thirty hectares of the property known as St Basil's with its superb view towards the mountains; and the splendid Villa Lawrence, preserved intact with its grounds and giant sequoia trees among the many subdivided properties, often still surrounded by their original walls and gates, which now enclose whole areas of the town. In the forty-five years of Pau's highest-flying days as a social and medical Mecca, these Anglo-Saxon families were as much a part of Pau as the locally born French themselves.

During those decades it was not only the British visitors and residents who worked to make their compatriots feel at home away from home. The local people, and particularly the mayor of the 1860s, the inspired Irish-descended Patrice O'Quin, went out of their way to attract and keep the best class of British guest, for such visitors, in addition to their own social and commercial worth, were a magnet to others who would come to Pau in the hope of meeting some scion of British society. Many of those who came thus were French, attracted by the fashion for all that was English, but there was also a strong supply of Americans who, unable to breach the bastions of London society, found that they had much more chance of 'breaking in' and meeting 'the quality' in a place like Pau.

O'Quin was elected to his post on a 'tourism ticket'. Under his mandate, and afterwards, Pau's first and almost only industry would be to attract and serve its visitors. And that meant first and foremost the British. The town underwent severe and serious reorganization and rebuilding. The streets were laid out in the British style, pavements were built, the drains were overhauled and sealed underground, the proliferating new hotels were brought up to higher standards, and a great plan for linking the whole frontage of the town facing the mountains with a huge scenic boulevard was put into action.

The view from the château gardens had often, over the

years, had the most lavish appreciation poured on it. Lamartine described it as 'the most beautiful view on land, as Naples is the most beautiful view on water' and a number of other writers had glorified it as the most outstanding prospect in Europe or even the world. O'Quin and his successors took that God-given view and used it. Paring off the backs of some of the large private gardens which bordered on the clifftop facing the mountains, they gradually acquired the land to build what would eventually become the Boulevard des Pyrénées, a wide carriageway running the whole length of the cliffline from the château gardens to the new public Parc Beaumont with its remarkable turn-of-the-century Casino buildings. From the whole of that boulevard the promenader could see the breathtaking view across the plains to the Pyrenees. It was the greatest glory of the town and a splendid tourist attraction.

The lovely Place Royale, the central square on the boulevard, surrounded by hotels, lined with trees and topped by the Théâtre St-Louis was the focus of the smart town's daily activities. On its very British bandstand, named for the composer Herr Rauski, the band could daily be heard turning out the tunes of 'Rule Britannia' and 'God Save the Queen' far more often than their French equivalents, as the fashionable folk strolled and socialized among the trees and tables. And beyond them, on a clear day, rose those incomparable mountains.

At one stage, in the early 1860s, nearly 20 per cent of the people in Pau were said to be British. And by the 1870s, the cartoonist Charles-Albert d'Arnoux could write:

> Pau is not a French town. Pau belongs quite obviously and clearly to Britain. The British have transplanted there their customs, their way of life and their pastimes, and they are unchallenged masters, by the strength of their banknotes – pounds and shillings are an artillery more invincible than anything from Krupp, Armstrong or Reffye.

O'Quin and Dr Taylor (who capitalized on Pau's vogue by moving cannily into speculating in real estate) and their native Béarnais colleagues succeeded in keeping their town to the fore for nearly half a century, before the fashion changed and took some of the smarter British trade away from them. The tale has it that it was Queen Victoria's fault. Her Majesty had accepted an invitation to come to Pau to present the 1889 trophy at the Pau Golf Club, but she did not turn up. On the way she had stopped at Biarritz and liked it so much that she did not continue her journey. Biarritz and the fashion for sea-bathing took over from Pau and *climatisme* as the 'way to do things', for where the queen led much of unthinking society would follow. Pau's loss was to be Biarritz's gain.

Although the greatest period of the British in Pau was over by the 1890s, the town still exerted a strong attraction for overseas visitors, with the subjects of the unkind queen still by far numerically and socially at their head. A wander through what remains of the old English Cemetery among the alleys of Pau's

Town Cemetery shows the crumbling graves of a wide mixture of the adoptive British and American Palois, who lived and died there in the later years of the nineteenth century and right on through to the 1940s. Many of the tombs have been destroyed to make place for newer burials, but alongside Dr Taylor and his wife lie such folk as Thomas Verner of the Bengal Lancers who was buried in 1889, the 4th Baron Kilmayne (1925), Major Gordon Hutton of the US Volunteers, Henry Fraser Curwen of Workington Hall, Cumberland (1900), Sir John Nugent, Bart, of County Waterford and his son who was killed at Gallipoli, Charles Wilkinson, JP for Westmorland and Kendal (1903), Mary Bosanquet of Hampton Court, Herefordshire (1914), the Reverend O.W. Morgan from Swansea (1934), Jane Gardner from New York (1881) who succeeded in becoming the Comtesse de Dion, and many, many others. Aline Coles and Edith Girdlestone raised a monument to their friend and housekeeper Hannah Wilkins in 1909; a tottering stele bears evidence that James Murphy, a Bombay civil servant, died at Eaux-Chaudes in 1876, aged 30; while a smashed stone records the 1924 wish of Winifred Hughes that Addy MacDonald of Glanranald, though gone, should not be forgotten. And among the endless rows, in a sober square of white marble covered with plain gravel, lies Mrs Stella Beatrice Cornwallis West, otherwise Mrs Patrick Campbell, and George Bernard Shaw's original Eliza Doolittle.

When Stella Campbell died in Pau in 1940 the town was little different in character from what it had been at the turn of the century. It was the warm, well-bred English-French town that both the English and French had made it into over nearly a century of happy cohabitation and mutual profit. Only after another war and the coming of oil, industry and the modern way of life would it begin to change into the city of today.

Although *Aspects of Love* is nominally set in the 1950s, David Garnett's Pau is very much the town of those pre-war years – the Pau of Addy MacDonald and Baron Kilmayne and the Reverend Morgan from Swansea, when the big villas lined the Boulevard des Pyrénées and you really could throw back the bedroom curtains and gaze out across the flat lands of Béarn at the loveliest view on earth. The days when the band played Gilbert and Sullivan on the bandstand, when the Hôtel Gassion welcomed reasonably rich and respectable Britons rather than the crowned heads it had courted in earlier days, and the English church and bank were still in business.

If the view of the Pyrenees from the great boulevard is to be rated among the most wonderful natural sights of the world, it has at least to share that rating with the views to be seen in and around the mountains themselves. The Pyrenean mountain range, running across the throat of the Iberian peninsula and forming a natural barrier between present-day Spain and France, along with its deep green foothills and its approaches, contains a whole host of glorious natural sights. Rare are the places where the modern world, with its aeroplane engine fac-

Les Eaux-Chaudes,
a spa town in the
Pyrenean foothills

tories or hydroelectric schemes, has infringed too aggressively
on the Béarnais landscape and on the life of the region.

Looking out from the great boulevard at Pau, 100 kilometres of mountains, from the Pic d'Arnelle far away in the east
to the Pic d'Arlas in the distant west, unfold in front of you,
sprouting up from the flat plains far beyond the nearby waters
of the Gave de Pau, fifty or sixty kilometres distant from the
town, in a burst of deep green hills clothed in lush, romantic forests, which finally turn to rock and snow some 1,500 metres
above the land.

On one hand the Valley of Ossau stretches up through the
vineyards of Jurançon – the home of the exceedingly fine,
attacking white wine of the region – to the towering Pic du Midi
d'Ossau. Beyond the picturesque fields and villages of the Gan
region with their odd cap-shaped roofs, the thermal spas of
Eaux-Bonnes and Eaux-Chaudes beloved of the Empress
Eugénie, and the farmhouses where the Pyrenean cheeses are
fabricated, the crest of this snowy high point of the range towers
nearly 3,000 metres above sea-level, among a whole court of its
lesser fellows.

In the other direction the Gave de Pau follows its course
down from the mountains, its white waters moving ener-
getically through the amazing greenness of the valley and its
acres and acres of vivacious cornfields. And along its valley
runs the road, past the old monastery of Lestelle-Betharram,
past Lourdes with its ancient castle perched on the hill and its
vast church – so out of scale with the rest of what is otherwise
really a very ordinary country town – past the spa of Argèles-
Gazost and steadily upwards through the forested foothills to
its end high above the plain.

There, in the heart of the mountains, are to be found such memorable sights as the magnificent Cirque de Gavarnie, a vast semi-circular wall of mountainous cliffs topped by snowy peaks from which a wild cascade of waterfalls tumbles downwards towards the plains. The white water and the white snow against the starkness of the grey-black rock-faces and the irrepressible greenness, which is such a characteristic of the Pyrenean landscape, make a dramatic and unforgettable picture.

David Garnett once made his way there during a motoring holiday, and although not everything in what his companion, author Mina Curtiss, called 'lovely, un-tourist-ridden southwest France' pleased him – the Hôtel de France at Pau was 'dear and too big' and Lourdes 'looked like an Amusement Park' – he could not fail to be impressed by the journey to Gavarnie and the splendour and romance of the mountains.

> . . . we drove past meadows, mauve with autumn crocus in bloom, high up through the Pyrenees to the Cirque de Gavarnie. On muleback we rode up to this spectacular natural amphitheatre with its snowcapped mountains and massive cascades. Above it, too high for us to reach, is the Brèche de Roland, a cleft in a wall eighty feet thick which the legendary Roland is said to have hewn with one blow of his sword Orandal, bestowed on him by Charlemagne, according to one of the many legends.
>
> Mina Curtiss, *Other People's Letters*

Of course, it has not changed. Even the mules (which I think are actually Pyrenean mountain horses) are still there, ferrying customers the four kilometres from the town of Gavarnie to the Cirque.

But Gavarnie is not an isolated splendour. Whichever way you turn there are more beautiful and striking scenes of nature, plunging gorges and rivers – such as the dizzying drop over the Pont Napoléon at the deliciously shabby spa town of Luz-St Sauveur – or green highlands reaching up to rocky cols bearing the names made famous by the Tour de France bicycle race – the angry-looking Col d'Aubisque, the steep green Col du Soulor and the lofty Col du Tourmalet, all naked in the summer air but metres deep in snow once the winter months arrive.

The signs of real country life are there too, providing a gentle antidote to the prettily faded tourist towns of yesteryear and the overwhelmingly romantic natural atmosphere. There are cows and pigs and sturdy mountain horses, fields full of rolls of mown hay alongside the old stone barns and walls of the high country farms, and placards advertising farm-made cheese or honey, or Pyrenean dogs for sale. But, even in the face of these witnesses to hard farm labour, there is something indestructibly idyllic about these mountains. Many is the occasion when you feel that, but for a distant tractor, you might be half a century back in time; that Rose and Alex might appear over the next rise on their way to picnic among the rocks and the trees, running along the grass together with the silhouette of the mountain range carved out against the sky behind them.

The Making of the Musical

Many is the musical stage show that has remained two, three or even four years in its creators' brains, gradually and gently being evolved into that finished article which would ultimately be presented before an audience in the theatre. There are rather fewer that have had a gestation period lasting an entire decade. *Aspects of Love* is one of them.

David Garnett's twenty-five-year-old novel was initially brought to the attention of Andrew Lloyd Webber and his collaborator, Tim Rice, as long ago as 1979, when a friend of Rice's, who was involved in the film industry, mentioned the book to him as possible material for cinematic treatment. Both writers read, and were fascinated by, Garnett's rich yet unextravagant tale of different aspects of love in a warm climate and, when the proposed film faded away, somehow the characters of *Aspects of Love* did not. They persisted in the composer's mind, mostly hidden away in a corner, where they did not impinge on day-to-day life and his hugely busy and highly successful programme of work, but they would pop intrusively to the fore on regular (and sometimes inconvenient) occasions, almost as if they were demanding to be dealt with.

Finally, a couple of years after the writers of *Jesus Christ Superstar* had originally been introduced to the book, this intermittent haunting had its effect. Lloyd Webber and Rice decided that they would try and see if *Aspects of Love* had the potential for development into a stage musical. Given the style and tone of their previous works, it might have seemed an unlikely choice. After the joyfully contemporary fable of *Joseph and the Amazing Technicolor Dreamcoat*, and the punchy, modern rock opera treatment of *Jesus Christ Superstar*, the pair had most recently had enormous international success with their vividly dramatic *Evita* – an aggressively operatic musical, which dealt with people in the clutches of powerful passions and power politics in a searingly incisive and expansive way. The last thing that their now vast public would expect from them as a follow-up would be a musical based on this delicately stylish period piece with its gentle, sunny colouring, its intimate, private relationships and its inherently unspectacular story.

However, since the production of *Evita*, Lloyd Webber had made an interesting and exciting excursion, in collaboration with lyricist Don Black, into an unaccustomed area – that of the characterized song-cycle. Together, the pair had written a series of songs for solo female voice, the principal number and title of which was 'Tell Me on a Sunday', which unfolded, song by song, the various – and mostly unfortunate – episodes in the tragi-comic love life of its singer. First performed and recorded by Marti Webb as a concert item, it ultimately made its way to the stage as the first part of the entertainment *Song and Dance*, but at this point in time it existed simply as a selection of songs, linked by the character of the performer.

This piece of work had released its composer's talents and thoughts into a new area of writing, an area far from the expansively theatrical mode of his previous theatre successes; and it occurred to Lloyd Webber – before any idea had been conceived of putting 'Tell Me on a Sunday' on to the dramatic stage – that this more personal and introspective kind of writing could be deeply effective in a full-scale musical. If, that is, a suitable subject was available. It was inevitable that these thought processes should coincide with the ever-present *Aspects of Love* characters. Was this, perhaps, what they would be good for, and what would be good for them?

The first effort at the making of a musical of *Aspects of Love* began as a very genuine one. The writers contacted Garnett, who was delighted, if rather incredulous, at the prospect of his book being 'operaticized' by the creators of *Jesus Christ Superstar*, and arrangements began for the stage rights in the novel to be assigned to Lloyd Webber and Rice. The collaborators even headed for France and steeped themselves in the atmosphere of the tiny village of Eugénie-les-Bains, to the north of Pau, which had been turned into a fashionable spa in the days of the Empire because of the favour shown to it by the Empress Eugénie, wife of Napoleon III.

The village might seem to have been a curious venue to choose for their research, given that the action of *Aspects of Love* takes place in the rather different countryside to the south of Pau, but nowadays Eugénie-les-Bains has found an even more attractive commodity than its healthy waters to keep the visitors coming its way. In 1974 the chef Michel Guérard installed himself at 'Les Près d'Eugénie', turned it into a luxurious hotel, and made it the base for his 'invention' of the *nouvelle cuisine* fad, which would soon flood the world with minute portions of artistically and expensively displayed mincings of food. At this time 'Les Près d'Eugénie' was at the height of its fame, and it is not surprising that the tables and cellars of Guérard's establishment proved more of an attraction to the two young men than getting down to work on the new musical. No doubt David Garnett, that confirmed gourmet, would thoroughly have approved.

And so, having made its first and not very whole-hearted attempt to clamber off the printed page and into the musical theatre, *Aspects of Love* the musical descended once more into literary limbo. But not for very long. Those characters still had

Trevor Nunn and
Andrew Lloyd Webber

the habit of making their presence felt, even when Lloyd Webber's mind was wholly involved in something else. In the spring of 1981, that something else happened to be *Cats* but, in spite of the daily multitude of problems which surrounded the construction of the show, which was to turn out to be the most successful musical ever staged, he was already thinking ahead to his next work. And *Aspects of Love* was still there, forcing itself on him as a contender. There was nothing for it; it simply had to be exorcised. He would have to have another try.

Cats had lined up an adventurous production team, headed by director Trevor Nunn, the artistic director of the Royal Shakespeare Company. It was Nunn, in tandem with choreographer Gillian Lynne, who evolved into their final form the slick series of song-and-character-dance routines of which the show was constructed; but he also displayed a hitherto unsuspected gift as a lyricist, when he compiled, from fragments of Eliot's writing and from his own imagination, the last-minute lyrics for the show's most famous number, the wistful and heart-rending 'Memory'. Here was what the Victorians, in their wisdom, used simply to call a 'man of the theatre', someone who could turn his hand skilfully to many or all areas of a production. One day, during rehearsals, Lloyd Webber put a book into the director's hand. It was *Aspects of Love*. Attempt number two at turning Garnett's novel into a stage show was under way.

During 1983 Lloyd Webber and Nunn worked on a synopsis and some trial sections for an *Aspects of Love* musical, and in September it was decided to give the work-in-progress a trial run. Lloyd Webber had constructed a small theatre from an old chapel in the grounds of his Hampshire country home in Sydmonton. There, each year for several years past, he had staged a small festival, at which it had become a habit to perform, for a group of close friends and colleagues, some of his recent compositions that had not yet been unveiled before the general public. In such a way 'Tell Me on a Sunday' had been given its first performance there, as had the first of the songs based on T. S. Eliot's *Old Possum's Book of Practical Cats*, which had ultimately become the basis for *Cats*; the earliest sketches for *Starlight Express*; and the score for Rod Argent's musicalization of the Kit Williams treasure-hunt book *Masquerade*, which was subsequently staged at the Young Vic.

This year, the songs created about and around *Aspects of Love* shared the bill with some of the newer pieces that had been written for *Starlight Express*. Marti Webb, who had created 'Tell Me on a Sunday', and Paul Jones, the pop-singer turned actor who had recorded the role of Peron in *Evita*, performed the pieces. The 'cabaret' *Aspects* went down well, but the limelight and the writers' attention were heavily focused on the *Starlight Express* material, for that show had already been scheduled for production with Nunn as director, and the first stages of the long and complex route that were to lead to putting it on the stage were already under way.

So, once again, *Aspects of Love* went into limbo. This time, however, the situation was rather different. This time Garnett's characters had found themselves a voice, they had been given a real chance to climb off the printed page and into the theatre – but either it was not quite the right voice, or else the whole idea was itself a wrong one, for, in the experiment of putting the piece to music, it had been found that they had not conveyed the essence of the work in the way that they wanted to. If anything was to become of the musical *Aspects of Love* there was some re-thinking to be done.

The limbo into which the piece now disappeared was a very much darker one, as both Lloyd Webber and Nunn were committed to other projects, although Nunn – returning to the original and more obvious possibility of an *Aspects of Love* film – had shown interest in the cinematic rights to the book. The story and everyone in it now came the nearest they had yet come to disappearing back between their Chatto & Windus covers for good. As for the musical contents of the 'cabaret', over the years they were dispersed, as Lloyd Webber remoulded some of the most attractive thematic material from the exercise into pieces for his later shows. Music from one number became *The Phantom of the Opera*'s 'Music of the Night', while another resurfaced as the theme song for the television series *Executive Stress*.

Nunn returned to the Royal Shakespeare Company and, for the time being, with *Aspects of Love* seemingly shelved for good, he and Lloyd Webber followed different paths. Inevitably, Lloyd Webber ventured away into further unexplored pastures. Among the large periods of time which he devoted over the next few years both to the proliferating productions of his earlier successes, first in America, and then in all corners of the globe, and to the growth – and ultimately the public launch – of the Really Useful Company, he found time to compose a full-scale Latin requiem mass. This is surely the only mass in history to have placed a song – Sarah Brightman and Paul Miles-Kingston's soaring soprano duet version of the 'Pie Jesu' – in the hit parades. The requiem was featured in a series of international concerts, before Lloyd Webber turned to working on the grandiose, classically romantic piece that had so long been awaited from him: *The Phantom of the Opera*.

By the time *The Phantom of the Opera* reached its triumphant opening night at London's Her Majesty's Theatre, more than four years had passed since anything practical had been done about *Aspects of Love*. Even in those circles which are always so very sure they know everything about everything on the London theatrical scene, it had ceased to be chattered about. The gossips had had their certainties about it shaken twice already. Now it seemed that, given Tim Rice's productions of *Blondel* and *Chess*, the *Aspects of Love* idea would be the only subject that had been mooted in the days of the Lloyd Webber–Rice partnership which would never make it to the stage.

The gossips, like everyone else, had, however, counted without the novel's tenacious attraction for Lloyd Webber. *Aspects of Love* had seemed a particularly interesting subject to him eight years before, and eight years, in spite of two unconsummated attempts to bring the piece to life, had not lessened his convictions. Surely, what was a good idea in 1979 was still a good idea in 1987? He was now convinced, too, that he knew what had been wrong with the angle he and Nunn had taken on their previous attempt – they had tried to make their *Aspects of Love* too big. Too big in all-round conception, and, on his own side, too big in musical ideas and even, perhaps, in melody. The very fact that the soaring vocal line of 'Music of the Night' – admittedly in a newly arranged and orchestrated form – had become so successful and important a part of the deeply romantic fabric of the period drama of *The Phantom of the Opera* made him realize its questionable suitability for the much less richly flavoured *Aspects of Love*.

Another element also joined the conspiracy to bring *Aspects of Love* back to the forefront of Lloyd Webber's mind. Ever since the first, flamingly extravagant production of *Jesus Christ Superstar*, his stage works had received large and often spectacular productions – the stark drama and green satire of *Evita*, with its large chorus of singers and dancers and its even larger principal characters, the rubbish-heap full of innumerable dancing *Cats* in their slinky catsuits, the high-tech wizardry of *Starlight Express*, the vast romantic glories of *The Phantom of the Opera*. Even the intimate 'Tell Me on a Sunday' had somehow been given a spectacular dimension by the imaginative design and staging lavished on it on the sizeable stage of the Palace Theatre. Now he knew that he wanted to do something smaller, something more personal, where the spectacular and novelty elements were not as important, the number of cast smaller, the whole scale less vast. Something where the focus was first and foremost on the characters, their story, their relationships, their words and, of course, their music. Needless to say, it needed a story and characters to fit. Nothing like *The Phantom of the Opera*. A story like . . . well, a story like *Aspects of Love*.

Just as the production of *Cats* had provided the stimulus and the opportunity for the collaboration which had set in motion the last attempt to get *Aspects of Love* on the musical road, so *The Phantom of the Opera* provided the newest occasion. During the production period, the topic of the novel and Lloyd Webber's continuing interest in it came up in conversation between the composer and Charles Hart, the lyricist of *The Phantom of the Opera*. Hart, intrigued to investigate a book which was able to have such an enduring effect on a man who had the whole world of literature to choose from, promptly went in search of a copy. Liberty's book department yielded a paperback edition and, over the days that followed, Hart trundled the little book around in his briefcase, taking what chances arose to read and re-read its content. It was still in his briefcase when the *Phantom* team gathered together for the recording sessions of the original cast album.

Lloyd Webber was quick to spot the familiar paper cover and to register his young collaborator's interest. It proved to be the catalyst he needed to start his mind clicking along once again on the tracks of *Aspects of Love*. Maybe now was the time to have another try. To see if something really could be made of it. But as what? Was it a stage musical? Or was it perhaps, given the very cinematic style of narration used in many parts of the book, really more suitable material for an original musical film? One way or another, he was as convinced as ever that it ought to be something. Maybe if he started work that something would eventually become evident.

With a fresh mind to use as a sounding-board, he launched into the first stages of *Aspects of Love* Mark III. One by one, the many ideas that he had gathered and developed over the years were brought up and passed in review, as one discussion over dinner led to another and another. The results of all the dining and discussing were positive enough to keep the project alive and, when Lloyd Webber left London for his home in the sunshine of Cap Ferrat, on the French Mediterranean coast, Hart soon followed him south for more *Aspects of Love* sessions.

The general feeling at this stage favoured making the piece into a film, but nothing at all was certain, nothing at all concrete. The two men talked, read, scribbled a bit, and talked some more, as spring in the south of France moved on towards summer, tossing around fresh ideas on the form and shape the film or show might take, and shaping and reshaping the out-

Don Black

Charles Hart

lines and synopses developed both from the original book and from all the previous outlines and synopses.

The result of much thirsty labour and many late-night sessions ultimately emerged – a scene-by-scene synopsis of the proposed piece, carefully following the main strands of the book while telescoping some of its less practical and less attractive details, and annotated in parallel with notes on the musical and thematic patterns and progressions which the composer envisaged. There it was. Did they have something? Would it work? After much thought, Lloyd Webber decided that it would work well enough; as a starting point at least. It was time to end the exploratory stages and begin actually to put words and music on paper.

Hart, already deeply immersed in the project, would obviously be part of the writing team, as he had been on *The Phantom of the Opera*. As the third member of that team, Lloyd Webber approached Don Black, the lyricist who had served him so exceptionally well with the lyrics for 'Tell Me on a Sunday', his most intimate and personal work to date.

From June 1987 the work sessions at Cap Ferrat thus became three-handed affairs; now it was not just ideas that were going into the Mediterranean melting pot, but singable words and playable notes. The skeleton synopsis of scenes and story – which was still to undergo a number of structural changes during the coming months – was at last being clothed in 'show'. The basic elements were being built up bit by bit into a score.

The synopsis was, of course, not the only starting point. Neither the words nor the music were taken wholly off the top of the writers' heads. The lyricists, determined to be faithful to the novel, had David Garnett's dialogue to refer to, both for the structure of the story and also for important phrases and the right colour of language in weaving their songwords. Lloyd Webber, in turn, had stored in his head a number of tunes in his most effective vein which had not been happily placed on their first airing and which were still waiting for the opportunity to blossom into full-blown songs under the right conditions and in the right show.

Several such melodies had been used the previous year in a light-hearted and quickly put-together musical piece called *Cricket*, which Lloyd Webber had been asked to write by Prince Edward for Her Majesty The Queen's sixtieth birthday. On this occasion he had invited Tim Rice, the cricket-mad partner of his débuts, to collaborate on an idea they had mulled over some years before. Staged privately at Windsor Castle and subsequently at Sydmonton, *Cricket* had proved to be plenty of fun, but its rather light, burlesque style and story, and some purposely jaunty and sometimes tongue-in-cheek band and harmony writing, had served to obscure, behind considerations of character and comedy, musical lines that had genuine lyric beauty and effectiveness. *Cricket* was a jolly little *pièce de circonstance*, a one-act musical comedy with few or no pretensions to a significant future, but underneath all the fun it was clear that those melodies were good. This was a case where the good ought not to be allowed to die young. Some of them, suitably developed and adapted, were already earmarked to fit the situations and characters of *Aspects of Love*.

Work sessions stretched on through days, nights and then weeks as the three writers, gathered round the piano, shaped the various sections of the score ready to be set with words. The cryptic notes pencilled on the synopsis by the composer began to develop into music, as Lloyd Webber gave melodies to the elements of the score which had previously been marked down only under such names as 'Love-Hymn', 'Damn-the-Boy Theme', 'Love Duet', 'Pacifying Theme', 'Renunciation Theme', 'Pyrenees Tune', 'Souvenir Léger' or 'Ghost Motif', and then set to developing them along the lines which he had sketched out on the synopsis.

Some musical lines underwent considerable development. A phrase or a fragment of a theme might be developed, first through a recitative section, modulating, building, being varied and then finally bursting into its fully fledged form in a full-blooded song section. At the other end of the scale, some melodies or groups of notes were never allowed to reach that sort of sung-out apotheosis, but were tweaked into the score, here and there, linking the scenes or bringing back memories of earlier themes.

In composing a score it is not in any way logical that the first song to be written should be the song which opens the show. In the case of the new *Aspects of Love*, however, that was indeed the case. From a long way back it had been planned that the musical should begin with a big, expressive song; a number for male voice sung, perhaps, by an unidentified soloist, who was not otherwise part of the show's story, and describing in the most desperately yearning terms a man and a life consumed and coloured by a great and unfulfilled love. A song which distilled the essence of the novel and of the show.

The melody that Lloyd Webber selected for this crucial number – the number which would set the play on its way with all wheels rolling – was a particularly beautiful one which he had been nursing for some time. It had previously been envisaged as the starting point for an additional number for the Broadway production of *Starlight Express* and versions of it had, at various times, been set to words by all his four principal collaborators – Rice, Stilgoe, Nunn and Hart – but the result had never been truly 'right'. This time, however, he was convinced that the music had found its home – sung by a passionate human, rather than an anthropomorphic machine.

In contrast to some earlier efforts, 'Love Changes Everything', as the melody became known, was born with remarkable ease. Hart and Black's lyrics, as presented to the composer, and the layout of the music as originally planned, suffered barely a change between their first coming together and their final appearance.

Andrew Lloyd Webber

Love Changes Everything

Love,
Love changes everything:
Hands and faces,
Earth and sky,
Love,
Love changes everything:
How you live and
How you die.

Love
Can make the summer fly,
Or a night
Seem like a lifetime.

Yes, love,
Love changes everything:
Now I tremble
At your name.
Nothing in the
World will ever
Be the same.

The show's other important ballad, Rose's searing eleven o'clock piece, 'Anything But Lonely', had an equally unlikely genesis. Whereas the thematic stuff of 'Love Changes Everything' had almost been given to a *Starlight* train, the palpitating musical line of this powerful song had first been sung, albeit briefly, by a flannelled fool of a cricketer.

As in the case of 'Love Changes Everything', the building of 'Anything But Lonely' was the story of a melody come home. Music which had seemed amusingly tuneful and entertaining when sung by a cricketer standing at the crease, watching his girl go off with another man and wondering whether it were more important to get himself purposely bowled out and try to stop their departure, or to stick to his wicket like a man of cricketing honour, took on another dimension when turned into an expansive hymn on the desperation of being alone.

For the important 'Pyrenees Tune', the melody which illustrates the love between Alex and Rose, Lloyd Webber decided on a waltz theme – one of those gently winding French waltzes, which would first be heard floating in on a mountain breeze, sung in the untroubled treble of a shepherd boy, and which, after coming back, in larger or smaller fragments, to recall the passionate moments there had once been between the two, would reappear in its entirety sung by the young Jenny at the dawning of another love. The waltz tune itself was already there. It was one of the tunes that the composer had actually used in the *Aspects* cabaret. Now it was re-shaped and given a different feeling as the plaintive expression of youthful love, plaited into the other melodies and other loves of the show as 'Song of my Childhood'.

Like many other hard-worked lyrics, these charming words, which blended so well with their melody, never saw stagelight. By the time *Aspects of Love* reached production, 'Song of my Childhood' had become 'Chanson d'Enfance' and its lyrics were in French. Halfway through previews the shepherd boy went too, and the definitive version of the show gave the introduction of the wistful melody to Rose, lying on her stomach in the sunlight of a Pyrenean pasture and thinking of love.

Progress through the summer was slow, steady and significant, but there was much else besides the original lyric to 'Chanson d'Enfance' that came out of those days of work which did not survive until production. Some numbers were tried and quickly discarded; others were altered first a little, then more and more, until they had become virtually unrecognizable from the original. Even then the resulting piece was sometimes discarded. New material, revamped material, pieces of music and text worked over finely and painstakingly – nothing was sacrosanct, and anything and everything had to be tried.

Hart's spirits sank one day when he heard Lloyd Webber beginning to play about with one particularly attractive but familiar melody. Hart had nothing against the melody as such, quite the contrary, but it was a piece which had at four different stages been temporarily a part of *The Phantom of the Opera*. He

Anything But Lonely

Anything but lonely,
Anything but empty rooms.
There's so much in life to share –
What's the sense when no one else
    is there?

Anything but lonely,
Anything but only me.
Quiet years in too much space:
That's the thing that's hard to face,
And . . .

You have a right to go,
But you should also know
That I won't be alone for long.

Long days with nothing said
Are not what lie ahead –
I'm sorry, but I'm not that strong . . .

Song of my Childhood

Nothing's as hard
As what I must do,
Leaving here,
Leaving you.

Nothing's as deep
As the pain I'll know
Taking one last look
Before I turn to go.

Song of my childhood,
You'll call me back to these hills . . .
What could be sweeter?
Nothing is sweeter.

had already produced four different lyrics to it for four different situations, but the melody had never fitted satisfactorily in the show and, four times, it had been cut. Before long it was cut again. It did not fit *Aspects of Love* any more than it had fitted *Phantom*. But it had to be tried.

By the end of the summer, something like a rough-cut of a show had been assembled, but the following months held other preoccupations for both Lloyd Webber and Hart. *The Phantom of the Opera* was due to open in America and, therefore, the show's composer and lyricist were needed on the other side of the Atlantic. So, instead of forgathering for another sun-soaked writing (or, rather, re-writing) session in France, the *Aspects of Love* team set out for the United States. They could have been forgiven had the busy production period in New York temporarily put the thought of any other project right out of their minds but, once again, a major production did anything but put up the shutters where Lloyd Webber was concerned. On the contrary, the new staging of *The Phantom of the Opera* only served to stimulate the growth of *Aspects of Love*.

Maria Bjørnson, the designer, and Andrew Bridge, the lighting designer of *The Phantom of the Opera*, and Gillian Lynne, who was also in New York re-creating her original choreography for the earlier piece, were drawn into the *Aspects of Love* creative circle, together with Martin Levan, the sound designer. And the score, as it then existed, was for the first time put down on tape by the composer and a group of American singers, headed by *The Phantom of the Opera*'s Judy Kaye, in Lloyd Webber's apartment high up in the Trump Tower. By now, the idea of an *Aspects of Love* film musical was beginning gradually to fade away in favour of a stage show. Equally gradually, the project was beginning to move inexorably away from being 'possible' towards being 'very probable'. By the time *The Phantom of the Opera* had opened on Broadway and everyone was heading back to Britain, plans were being formulated to put *Aspects of Love* on to the stage.

At this time it was widely believed that Trevor Nunn would be directing the new Boublil/Schönberg musical, *Miss Saigon*. Therefore, because of the conflict in dates, Lloyd Webber had been actively courting the young English director, Nicholas Hytner, a rising star of the British opera. But the dates being considered proved impossible for Hytner, due to a previous commitment with the National Theatre. When subsequently Cameron Mackintosh announced that Trevor Nunn would not be directing *Miss Saigon*, Lloyd Webber once more turned to Nunn, with his aptitude for practical stage considerations and acutely analytical approach to the dramatic side of the play.

By early March 1988 they finally had a completed draft of the show ready. It was almost a year since Lloyd Webber and Hart had first begun their work together in France but, even so, what they now had, although substantial, was only a first draft. Much of what it contained would, indeed, make its way into the final staged version, for the broad outlines that had been estab-

Maria Bjørnson

Gillian Lynne

lished were solid, but there were still whole scenes which would
come and, more often, go in the second year of the preparation
of the piece for the theatre.

The next step was to look at the show in performance. Now
the Really Useful Group – the reorganized and public company
descendant of Lloyd Webber's original Really Useful Company, which had been responsible, alone or in partnership, for
the production of all his shows since *Cats* and a good number of
other people's as well – moved into action for the first time on
the new project. In the second week of April, studio and recording time was booked and preparations made for a full-scale
demonstration tape of the show's score, with a group of well-
known artists singing the principal roles. Gary Bond, nearly
twenty years earlier the original West End Joseph of *Joseph and
the Amazing Technicolor Dreamcoat*, took the role of George;
Michael Howe, the star of *Chess*, was Alex (no longer Alexis,
as in the book, the name having been given its *coup de grâce* by
Joan Collins and *Dynasty*); Claire Moore, who had succeeded
Sarah Brightman as Christine in *The Phantom of the Opera*, sang
the part of Rose; Maria Friedman played Giulietta; Paul
Bentley, who had starred in the Really Useful Group's production of the comedy *Lend Me a Tenor*, was Marcel; Mary
Millar, from the cast of *The Phantom of the Opera*, doubled as Elis-
abeth and circus *chanteuse*; and Diana Morrison, an eighteen-
year-old student at the Arts Educational School, sang the child,
Jenny.

Satisfied with the results of the demonstration, Lloyd Webber and the company then decided to take the show to the
second stage of performance – a staged production, which
would allow them to see how the broad lines of the show and its
characters worked. The performance was arranged for July at
Sydmonton with Trevor Nunn at its helm. Now, various problems which had not had to be faced before began to loom much
larger. The first of these was the casting. Most of the artists who
had sung the roles on the demonstration tape, while accurate
casting vocally, were by no means equally apt in other ways.
Although his acting credits displayed considerable versatility,
Bond was far from being able to appear in the role of a seventy-
year-old; Howe had not played (or wanted to play) a seventeen-
year-old since starring in *Grease* many years previously; and the
writers had very precise and difficult preconceptions as to what
they visualized their carefully recrafted Rose and Giulietta
being like, which threatened to turn the whole affair into a casting director's nightmare. It was a case, for these four parts at
least, of virtually starting from scratch.

The search continued for several weeks of auditions and re-
auditions. Finally four new performers were chosen to supplement Bentley, Mary Millar and Diana Morrison (whose
role had been divided in two for the stage so that she would not
have to play down to the age of ten or eleven) in the first staged
version of *Aspects*, as the show had inevitably become known in
showbiz short-talk. The dashing and suitably ageing Dinsdale

Landen, well-known as a leading actor but an unknown quantity as a singer, played George; Michael Ball, the youthful-looking leading man of *The Phantom of the Opera* was Alex; Susannah Fellows, the first alternate Evita and Bentley's co-star in *Lend Me a Tenor*, was Rose; and the young Anglo–Irish singer Graínne Renihan, Elaine Paige's replacement in *Chess*, tackled the strenuous song allotted to Giulietta. It was, the producing team knew, not wholly accurate casting, but there was no doubting the quality of the performers, and utter accuracy could wait until later. In the meantime, as the cast prepared their music – and Miss Renihan, who had suddenly discovered that she was going to be expected to speak, whispered helplessly to Landen, 'I'll teach you to sing if you'll teach me to act!' – Trevor Nunn was facing the other major problem: how to stage the show?

David Garnett's novel is full of quick scenes, sudden changes of focus, intimate moments which demand close-up attention, and those qualities had for so long been particularly influential in persuading the *Aspects* team into seeing the piece as material for a film rather than a stage show. Even when the stage won out over the cinema, that cinematic quality, which had appealed so much to Nunn, was maintained in the writing of the show. But how was this to be translated to the stage, particularly without the aid of considerable scenery and lighting effects?

Like the casting problem, this one was solved with a bit of 'for the meantime'. The Sydmonton *Aspects* would be a semi-staged one. The cast were seated in a row, with the chorus lined up behind them, rather like the soloists and choir members in an oratorio performance, moving forward as circumstances demanded to play out their scenes in front of the lines of chairs. Time, place and any other necessary bits of information were conveyed to the audience by captions, flashed on to a screen above the stage in the manner used for surtitles at the opera.

Only a few days of rehearsal were possible and, with most of the artists engaged in current West End shows, the performance itself was played on a Saturday morning, leaving them just enough time to scamper back to London and their respective matinées. But there was no need to make any kind of allowances – what came across from the stage to the audience of friends and colleagues gathered for the occasion was a warm and extremely personal musical play, melodious and moving, which lost nothing in its unconventional staging and occasionally off-line casting. It was by far the most finished piece of material that Lloyd Webber had ever put on stage at Sydmonton, and it was clear that the next step, a full-scale production, could be confidently and unhesitatingly envisaged. *Aspects of Love* was on. Well and truly on.

So while the Really Useful Theatre Company went into action, putting into motion all the different elements of the practical side of producing a major West End musical, the writers went back to the drawing-board to sum up the lessons learned from the Sydmonton production and to put them to effect in a new revision of the text. It was agreed that the larger outlines of the show had worked well, and that the characters and their delicate, complex mesh of relationships had, for the most, registered effectively and in the ways they were intended to, but there were areas that could be improved. Giulietta, for example, disappeared from the story after the first act scene in her studio and was not seen again until the wake. Would the audience have forgotten who she was? Some way needed to be found to keep her rather more visible in between . . . a reference here, a brief appearance there . . . and so it went on.

The text went under the microscope, with Nunn incisively directing the fining down and touching up operations, which can tear to tatters the hearts of a pair of lyricists who have already spent days and days doing their own fining down and touching up.

'The audience hasn't been told such-and-such, so they won't understand what happens in twenty pages' time . . . it needs a line . . . here . . . to tell them such-and-such.'

A piece of music is given a deft revision and the two lyricists go into a huddle, to emerge with something that both says what it needs to say with clarity and style and also fits the often complicated rhythmic patterns of the music.

'We need an extra syllable!' becomes a well-used cry.

'Well, there isn't a note for it, so you can't have it!' becomes an equally well-used reply.

But somehow, in the end, music and words come together to everyone's satisfaction and then it is on to the next one.

'I want to keep this line here . . . but I want to lose that one and that one, which go before it . . .'

'But that one *rhymes* with that one . . .!' from an anguished lyricist who can remember the hours spent arguing with his colleague over whether it was better to have 'and' or 'but' in the middle of the line that is about to be axed, and the ages spent sorting out two beautifully rhyming words that went dum-dum-DEE-dum at just the right time and place.

'I can't help that . . .' with a smile and a scalpel, and on to the next.

'Now what we want here, is something like this, only much better . . .' and out comes a line which fits the demands of the situation almost perfectly.

The lyricists, determined to do better, even if only on the principle that two heads are better than one, try a dozen different combinations before granting, a mite grudgingly, that it is not possible to do 'much better'.

'Why don't we try your line . . . for the moment?'

And so on to the next . . .

While this seemingly endless work progressed, advances were being made in other areas. Conductor and composer Michael Reed, the West End's senior, but youthful, theatre musical director, was appointed to the position of musical executive to the Really Useful Group, with the understanding that he would oversee the musical side of the production of *Aspects of Love* and conduct the early performances, as he had done for *The Phantom of the Opera*. David Cullen, who had, over the years, been involved in orchestrating almost all of Lloyd Webber's musicals, was signed to collaborate with the composer on the scoring of the latest in the line, alongside the rest of a creative team which had, bit by bit, been taken aboard during the time that *Aspects of Love* had been a-borning.

The names of Wyndham's, the Savoy and the Aldwych Theatres had been touted around among the *cognoscenti* as the intended home for the new show, and there were some taken-aback touters when it was discovered that the Prince of Wales Theatre had been booked. Immediately the wild and woolly stories that nowadays get attached to any new Lloyd Webber production, just as a century earlier they were eagerly pinned on any forthcoming Gilbert and Sullivan show, started to swirl around the gossips' circles. 'Did you know that they have paid *South Pacific* millions to get out of the theatre?' ran one version. 'Did you know that *South Pacific* was dying on its feet and they've paid them millions to stay until the end of the year, so that no one else can get into the theatre?' ran another, rather inconveniently opposite, one. Actually, the revival of *South Pacific*, which had recouped its investors' money in just a few weeks, had had a good run and, after twelve months in the West End, was preparing to go on the road. The theatre would be free.

In spite of the predictable demand for tickets that would arise as soon as the show was announced, there was no question of putting *Aspects of Love* into one of the West End's larger theatres. It had been specifically written on a smaller scale and in a more intimate style than a *Phantom* or a *Cats* and, even if the auditorium of the Theatre Royal, Drury Lane, could have been instantly and profitably filled for many months by those demanding tickets, the show itself would have been completely lost in the vastness of such a theatre, just as the sadly over-expanded version of *The Best Little Whorehouse in Texas* had been a few years previously.

The Prince of Wales, a well-situated, independent house, originally used for plays and revues, fitted the bill almost perfectly. Its 12.8 by 7.5-metre stage opening, although not particularly deep, seemed to provide a potential working surface which was capable of being manœuvred into the areas required. It had better sight-lines than many London theatres, its orchestra pit provided plenty of space for the fourteen-piece orchestra planned for the show, and its 1,133 seats, not significantly less than the 1,261 of Her Majesty's Theatre, provided both financial viability, which would have been risky in a smaller house, and a guarantee that audiences would not have to wait as long for tickets as they would have done in a house such as Wyndham's.

The Prince of Wales was secured from the second week of January 1989. That left what might have seemed like a luxurious three months for the necessary backstage alterations and

Michael Reed

David Cullen

adaptations to be made and for Maria Bjørnson's scenery to be installed. The first preview was scheduled for 31 March and the opening night for 12 April. And on Sunday 30 October 1988, the first advertisement for the show appeared in *The Sunday Times* and the *Observer*. The result was remarkable. From midnight – and even before – the lines to the all-night ticket booking agencies were simply taken by assault by theatre-goers in quest of tickets. Those who had had to wait for months and months to see *The Phantom of the Opera* were determined not to miss out this time.

By the time the first day of booking was over, an extraordinary £150,000 had been taken in ticket sales. But the surge did not let up, either at the theatre or at the agencies. In the first four weeks of booking over £2 million worth of tickets were sold and, by the time the New Year was rung in, the entire stock of the first six months of tickets available at the box-office had gone.

Judging by previous experience, it was decided not to announce the dates set aside for the first four previews, as there was always the chance of a possible delay and, rather than disappoint customers by a cancellation and arouse the ire of the professional previewers – whose wrath, when they are unable to see a new show before all their friends, often explodes in rude letters to the management and the papers – those dates were quietly held in reserve. It was clear that there would be no difficulty in finding a last-minute audience if and when a public performance was played. Even more cannily, the management booked a 'reserve' opening night, five nights later than the intended one – even to the extent of hiring the Waldorf Hotel for the post-première party on both nights. Just in case. It was a precaution unheard of in the West End theatre – but it was to turn out to be a very wise one.

And so, as applications for tickets continued to pour into the box-office at what was an almost unnerving rate, for a show which was still in the process of being written and designed and which was completely un-cast, the preparations for the production went steadily forward. Once again casting the show had to begin and, just as the second time had been so much more difficult than the first, the third and most important time was quite obviously going to be very much more difficult than the second. This time there would be no 'making do' in one area of an actor's abilities or suitabilities in order to accommodate special talents in another. This time the actors would have to fit their roles not only vocally and stylistically, but in age, shape, size and in any and every other department. They would have to fit impeccably the complex pictures of the characters which the creative team had built up over such a long period of development.

There was only one very important exception. The role of the child Jenny was the one part already cast. No one involved in the production could imagine the two halves of the role being played better than they had been at Sydmonton by thirteen-

The Prince of Wales Theatre

Zoe Hart

year-old Zoe Hart (who had previously accomplished the unlikely exploit of playing both little Cosette *and* the boy Gavroche
in *Les Misérables*) and by Diana Morrison.

Casting a major musical is inevitably a long, slow process.
An actor who seems like perfect casting to the director can be
vetoed by the musical director because he cannot reach the top
note; and when the music department gets excited over an actress who sings the music superbly, the director, in turn, too
often has to say 'no' because she does not fit the role as he envis-
ages it physically or in acting style. And there are plenty of
others, in between these more interesting contenders, who do
not arouse either department to enthusiasm, as the auditioning
process goes on through days and weeks to months, and
everyone begins to wonder if there is anyone remotely suitable left who has not yet been seen and rejected. In the end,
of course, you always get there, one way or another, and
everyone is happy.

Aspects of Love did, indeed, prove a more than usually difficult task. Weeks of auditions, both in London and New York,
passed and many fine performers came and went. Some of them
came back to audition again and again, as the creative team
gathered in their minds a group of actors and actresses whom
they admired and were keen to use in the show. But with the
Sydmonton team as the bench-mark for everyone's judgement
it was proving exorbitantly difficult.

The first adult role cast was scarcely a surprise. Finding a
strong, handsome young actor able to age convincingly from
seventeen to his mid-thirties and also able to cope with the ringing tenor lines of 'Love Changes Everything' and 'Seeing is
Believing' had been a tall order from the start. But both Nunn
and Lloyd Webber had worked with Michael Ball before: Nunn
had cast him in the juvenile lead of the original cast of *Les Misérables* with enormous success, and from there Ball had gone di-
rectly to *The Phantom of the Opera* to take over the role of Raoul,
as well as appearing alongside *Phantom* star Sarah Brightman in
a series of sell-out concerts of Lloyd Webber's music. The casting of Ball as Alex was so very obvious that, as in many such
cases, it was almost natural to resist it. Besides, Ball had
popped up out of the provinces for *Les Misérables*, and it was
always possible that there was another like him waiting to be
discovered. But the weeks of auditions had not thrown up a
challenger when Michael Ball was offered a role in the forthcoming musical, *Metropolis*. It was a case of grabbing him while
he was still available, or losing all chance of having him in the
show. Little discussion was needed, and Ball joined Miss Morrison and Miss Hart as the third member of the Sydmonton cast
to be confirmed for London.

The role of George was a special problem. A teenage tenor
was bad enough, but finding an actor able to play convincingly
a part ranging from sixty to eighty years of age, who had not
only the acting ability and the enormous charm necessary for
the role but also both a sufficiently warm and well-preserved

Diana Morrison

Michael Ball

singing voice and the musicality to tackle the often highly complex rhythms and intervals of the score, was a truly mighty task. Lloyd Webber had been heard to say on many occasions that George should be played by an actor with the charm and star quality of the late David Niven. The idea of the show, which was already sold out for weeks and months without the announcement of a single member of the cast, needing a star name in it may have seemed excessive, but Lloyd Webber – whose own name could have, and had, proven sufficient star-billing on its own – had often taken the insurance of having at least one famous name in the casts of his later shows. There had been David Essex in *Evita*, Brian Blessed, Judi Dench and then Elaine Paige, Paul Nicholas and Wayne Sleep in *Cats*, Michael Crawford in *The Phantom of the Opera* – and the shows had gained not only in public appeal but in theatrical quality as a result.

Enquiries were made about the availability of a number of well-known actors. Some were already booked for films or plays, others turned positively grey at the idea of trying to sing, and one or two, whose names could be found in the reference books as having appeared in musicals in their younger days, were not eager to admit that the reference books were right and now belonged to the 'I'm sorry, I only do Shakespeare [or films or whatever] these days' brigade. Some tested for the role, and practically all those who had qualms about their singing abilities proved to be justified.

Film and television star Roger Moore was not one of those who had appeared in a musical. But recently people had been trying to encourage him to do so. First of all there was an offer for him to star in *Ziegfeld* at the London Palladium, and then came an enquiry concerning *Aspects of Love*. Although he did not have the greatest confidence in his singing ability Moore was game to have a try. He flew to London, where he worked on the score of the show first with the Really Useful music department and then with the composer. The results were encouraging. The man might bashfully insist that he had never tried to sing – but the fact remained that he could hold a tune, and the advances that he had made over the few days of their work together encouraged everyone enormously. Everything else was perfect – he would make a marvellous George – and if he progressed as much again in the singing department during rehearsals as he had over the past few days, the result would be quite outstanding.

The announcement that Moore was to star in *Aspects of Love* caused something of a stir and the predictable '007 *sings*' kind of headlines in the newspapers. It also put additional pressure on the already heavily overstretched box-office, and the Really Useful Group judged it wise to advertise that Moore's presence was not guaranteed. It could hardly be. He had been signed only for a six-month contract – and all the tickets for the first six months of performances were already sold.

If this particular casting problem had cleared itself up

Roger Moore

satisfactorily, the same could not be said of the two leading
ladies' roles. Again and again the most promising of the talented actresses were called back, as Nunn and Lloyd Webber
tried to find what they envisaged as their Rose and Giulietta.
But no one was perfect and, as time was marching on and they
could not afford to be caught with no one for the roles, they
turned back to the results of their New York auditions. After all,
Alex and George were the essentially British characters of this
musical. Rose was French and Giulietta Italian. And although
the character of the novel and of the show was staunchly
English, these two were the exotic elements, the colourful Euro-
peans, of the piece.

Over the past decade, through the many productions in
which they had been involved there and the frequent auditions
held for their American companies, both Lloyd Webber and
Nunn had come to know Broadway and its players almost as
well as those of the British stage. With the help of New York
casting agents Johnson and Liff, they had auditioned during
the summer some of the artists who had impressed them over
recent years, with these new roles in mind.

Ann Crumb had recently worked for Nunn in the Broadway productions of *Les Misérables* and *Chess*, understudying
Judy Kuhn in the star role of Florence, as well as touring America both as Lloyd Webber's Evita and as Fantine in *Les Misérables*. Her pedigree was impeccable, and all the unpretentious
power and passion of Rose were there as well.

For Giulietta, the team selected another *Les Misérables* veteran in Kathleen Rowe McAllen. The stunning, dark and very
Italianate-looking Miss McAllen, then appearing as Cinderella
in a touring company of the musical *Into the Woods*, had already
visited London to play Fantine in *Les Misérables* for Nunn at the
Palace Theatre – owned by the Really Useful Group.

The two remaining principal roles, the smaller parts of
Rose's manager Marcel and the circus *chanteuse*, were, oddly
enough, the last to be cast. Sally Smith, a West End star at
seventeen in the musical *Marigold* and most recently seen in
Follies, was cast as the singer and, after months of looking at
other actors, Paul Bentley, who had played Marcel both on the
recording and at Sydmonton, was finally offered the part. The
creative team had tried hard to find someone who fulfilled their
original picture of Marcel – a sweaty, obese and effeminate
Frenchman – and who still performed the role as well as Bentley had done in the first two versions. They did not find one
and so, rather than compromise on the side of quality performance, Marcel ended up being played by a slimmish, masculine
and unsweaty Englishman slightly padded, accented and be-
spectacled for the occasion.

By the time the new year dawned, the budding musical was
well and truly on its way. Designs were coming off paper and
into existence, the final refining of text and score was under
way, and David Cullen was hard at work with the composer,
transforming the orchestral sound of the piece from that of

Paul Bentley

Ann Crumb (*opposite top*)
Kathleen Rowe McAllen (*opposite centre*)
Sally Smith (*opposite bottom*)

Creative consultation: Lloyd Webber, Hart,
Nunn and Black

the small group used at Sydmonton to that of the fourteen-piece orchestra planned for the full stage production.

On 30 January 1989 the public got their first taste of the music from *Aspects of Love* when a recording of 'Love Changes Everything', sung by Michael Ball, was released. The reaction to the song was stunning. Immediately following its release, it began a cavalcade up the British hit parades, and four weeks later it had reached the number two position, the best performance by a show song in several years and its composer's tenth top-ten single from nine shows.

On the same day that Ball's recording was released, the cast came together for their first rehearsal, far from the bright lights of Shaftesbury Avenue and the Strand and the gutted Prince of Wales Theatre, in a community centre which one of the cast described as being 'in one of those inner-city housing estates where the washing is always hanging out of the windows and over the balconies'. This was to be their home for the first six weeks of the scheduled ten weeks of the rehearsal period. While Gillian Lynne started to stretch and bend a cast that included scarcely a trained dancer in its ranks into the physical shape needed to tackle what was to come, the music department would work with each cast member, individually and as a whole, to teach the entire score and achieve the very best results. Arranged around this would be all the costume fittings and press interviews. It was against this background that Nunn began to build the show.

At the end of six weeks and on the Friday, for the first time,

Far from the bright lights: rehearsal days

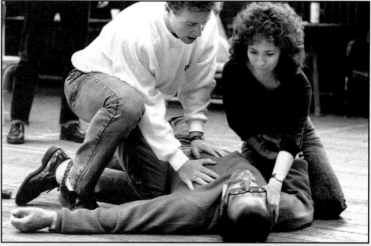

the show was given a run-through from top to bottom. It went splendidly and everyone was delighted. Things were in good shape and it was time to move into the theatre on Monday. But when Monday came, it was back to the community centre. The theatre was not ready. And so another week went by.

The next Monday, alas, had its own surprises in store. The first came when Roger Moore tendered his resignation. In spite of all the progress he had made, he was prohibitively uneasy about the musical part of his role and, after six weeks of rehearsals, had decided that he was not going to get any less uneasy in the weeks leading up to opening night. So, he thought, best to go now while there was sufficient time to find a replacement, rather than two days before the première.

Fortunately for all concerned, the management had already contracted a 'cover' for the role, in the event of Roger Moore suffering a physical or vocal injury which might have necessitated him missing a performance. Australian Kevin Colson, the London star of *Cabaret* and *Robert and Elizabeth* and a series of other musicals in the 1960s, had lately made a return to the stage after a number of years in business. He had most recently created the role of Walter de Courcey in *Chess* at the Prince Edward Theatre, and he still had a few weeks to play in the show (having swapped his original role for that of the expansive Russian Molokov) before taking up his role as 'cover' and ultimately succeeding Roger Moore as George in *Aspects of Love*. The management of *Chess* agreeably released him, and rehearsals were able to continue with much less upset than would normally have been the case, and with a George who already knew the role.

Kevin Colson

Rehearsals in the Prince of Wales Theatre bar (*opposite*)

In rehearsal: Ann Crumb as Rose

This black Monday, however, had not yet finished with *Aspects of Love*. That night was the first technical run-through of the show and it was to hold its own store of horrors. Suffice it to say that, as the performers struggled through their text and music, almost every major piece of scenic material refused to do what it was supposed to do and, as a *coup de grâce*, a rogue chip in the computerized lighting board went berserk and wiped out the entire lighting plot of the show, which had been laboriously set and stored there for what should have been eternity.

There was nothing to do but abandon the rehearsal. The technical staff went to work at full speed, spending every waking hour of their lives in the theatre (and there were not many sleeping ones during that week), trying to get the stage and the lighting back to the state they were supposed to be in. The cast, unable to work on the stage yet again, found they could not even get back into the community centre, which had duly taken in its next tenant, and for the rest of the week rehearsals were conducted wherever sufficient square inches of flat ground could be found – among *The Phantom of the Opera* sets at Her Majesty's Theatre or those of *Les Misérables* at the Really Useful Group's Palace Theatre, in the basement of the Theatre Royal, Drury Lane – nightly inhabited by the she-wolf of Australia, Dame Edna Everage – in tiny studios, or, as a last resort, in the bar of their own theatre, so near to, yet so far from, the stage they had expected to be working on a fortnight earlier.

By the following Monday – the eighth of their rehearsal period – it was safe to go back on the stage, and now at last the show started to come together. The technicalities of the staging of the show, which, unlike the actors, had not been rehearsed solidly for nearly two months, had to be given their share of attention – not just the major, obvious problems and potential problems, but such details as the excision of the smoke screens, intended for the station and circus scenes, due to Ann Crumb's allergy to the smoke; or the trimming of the vast fingers of tree-branches, whose weight was a worry, and which threatened to catch in the other scenery on the minutely spaced bars of the scenic grid. Bit by bit, however, everything began to slip into smoothish action, the orchestra – which had already taken many band calls – arrived, and finally, at the beginning of the ninth week of preparations, the great day came when it was possible actually to run through the whole of the first act, with all the music and scenery intact.

Later in the week the second act got the same treatment. On the Friday night everybody staggered through the first dress rehearsal. The next night went better, in fact sufficiently well for a few invited guests to be brought in for a third run-through on the Monday, which went pleasingly well. In spite of everything, and at least a week short of planned rehearsal on stage, *Aspects of Love* was going to be able to play its first preview performance as advertised.

At that first preview everything that had gone so right the previous night went wrong. There was still a lot of work to be

On to the stage ... into the costumes ...

In rehearsal: Michael Ball (Alex) and Kathleen Rowe McAllen (Giulietta) (*opposite top*); Ann Crumb (Rose) and Paul Bentley (Marcel) (*opposite bottom*)

done to get the immensely complex technical side of the show to perform reliably, and some of this 'working' also called for alterations in the text. So while the backstage teams beavered away on the various aspects of the physical production, the show itself was undergoing regular alterations, extensions and cuts. Many of these were minor, but even a small alteration in such a piece can often require much adjustment from cast and crew alike. One alteration was the complete cutting of a scene. And, by the laws which govern such things, it had to be a scene which included one of the largest and most expensive property pieces in the whole show – a model of a 1940s' Rolls-Royce car. Since there was insufficient floor space, this great piece of equipment had been stored suspended above the wings, and nearly everyone backstage, who had warily eyed the car dangling above their heads, was not sorry to see it go.

As the early previews played, the technical side of the show regularly began to run more smoothly, while the performers daily rehearsed the latest round of minor changes to the usual run of minor disasters – one actor took a tumble into the orchestra pit and narrowly avoided ending up on the harp; a sound operator vanished through a hole in the stage in front of Ann Crumb's eyes and feet, and emerged with a broken ankle; Gillian Lynne received a property hay bale on her head, as she watched the show from the wings; and Sally Smith lost her voice and had to take several nights off. But the show itself was moving onwards and upwards all the time.

What soon became obvious, however, was that it would not be as properly pinned and polished as everyone would have liked by the announced opening night. It was time for Plan B. Even though the opening night seating plan, a vastly complicated piece of diplomatic jigsawing, had been completed, the tickets had not been released to the première audience, so it was decided that *Aspects of Love* would open not on 12 April but on the 'reserve' first night, five days later.

The more vulturish of the popular papers, which had gleefully seen in Moore's departure an opportunity to begin baleful stories of impending disaster, leaped into printed speculation at this wonderful new sign that all might not be well. Spectators from the previews who would make nicely negative quotable quotes had the thrill of seeing themselves and their words in the papers, or of hearing themselves on the radio, in palpable defiance of the tacit agreement between producers and press organizations banning critical comment of a show before its opening. Whether it was simply a love of the mediocre which made these papers feel that Lloyd Webber's impressive run of successes had earned him their opposition, or the fact that *Aspects of Love* had, owing to its vast advance booking, needed to take only a tiny amount of paid newspaper advertising, whether it was good old-fashioned if-it's-British-how-can-it-be-good masochism or simply that tired and phoney old newspaperman's excuse 'but it's a good story' which was the basis of it all, there was no doubt that most of the press gossips were, for some reason, gunning against the show. However, the endless ringing of the box-office phones seemed to indicate that few members of the public were taking much notice, and the switch had in fact affected nobody.

The show itself continued to be readied, with all kinds of changes to score and script proceeding every day. The order of scenes in the first act underwent some changes, and a few more conventional finishes and pauses were put into the written-through score to allow the audience to applaud its fill. When Queen Elizabeth and Prince Philip attended a charity preview, they saw a version of the show which had taken in eight new alterations that day, including a sizeable piece of fresh solo material for Giulietta, and it was with great relief that everyone watched a performance which was concluded without a hitch. Those of the newspapers which reported the event, however, preferred to highlight, with a vivid flight of imagination, 'Lesbian scene cut for Queen'!

Many of the guests for the originally intended first night took their seats for what was now officially a preview, and thus the creators and cast of the show experienced what was almost a dress-rehearsal first night, while still working daily on improvements. It was a landmark performance, however. For the first time the show was played to what was not largely a 'professional preview audience' and the difference in reaction to the show was noticeable. The laughs, the sighs and the applause were suddenly coming in nearly all the intended places. It was no coincidence that very shortly after that night something clicked. All the work of the last months suddenly came together, and although the team would probably want to do some further fine-tuning in the months to come, they had a finished show just a couple of days before the first full-scale performance.

On the first night, the new musical went splendidly. And the rest, as somebody almost said, is continuing history.

THE GUARDIAN

'It is an unusual musical for this day and image: one that explores the human heart rather than the possibilities of hi-tech scenery. And, at his best, MrLloyd Webber shows a capacity to reach emotions that other composers do not touch.'

Michael Billington

FINANCIAL TIMES

'You will want to see this show not because of its showbiz hype, but because there are new creative forces at work here which may yet define the lyric theatre of the future.'

Michael Coveney

INTERNATIONAL HERALD TRIBUNE

'Like most great musicals *Aspects of Love* manages at the same time to be both nostalgic and barrier-breaking, and in that haunting score by Lloyd Webber and Don Black and Charles Hart are moments of classical brilliance ...'

'At the end of what has unquestionably been the richest musical decade in British theatrical history, *Aspects of Love* comes as both a crowning achievement and an intriguing pointer to the future.'

Sheridan Morley

THE DAILY TELEGRAPH

'Lloyd Webber's best so far'

Charles Osborne

DAILY MAIL

'Lloyd Webber dares and comes up with yet another winner.'

Jack Tinker

DAILY MIRROR

'The most romantic show in town is also the most triumphant.'

Hilary Bonner

'Love, love changes everything . . .'

Overleaf:

'Parlez-vous français? Je suis sad.' A love affair begins over a glass of Armagnac (Rose and Alex) (*top left*)

'Seeing is believing, and in my arms I see her . . .' (*bottom left*)

'A love affair is not a lifetime.' (George and Giulietta) (*top right*)

'Damn the boy's schoolboy antics!' – at the sculpture exhibition in Paris (*bottom right*)

'Whenever we see those mountains we will think of me and you' (*main picture*)

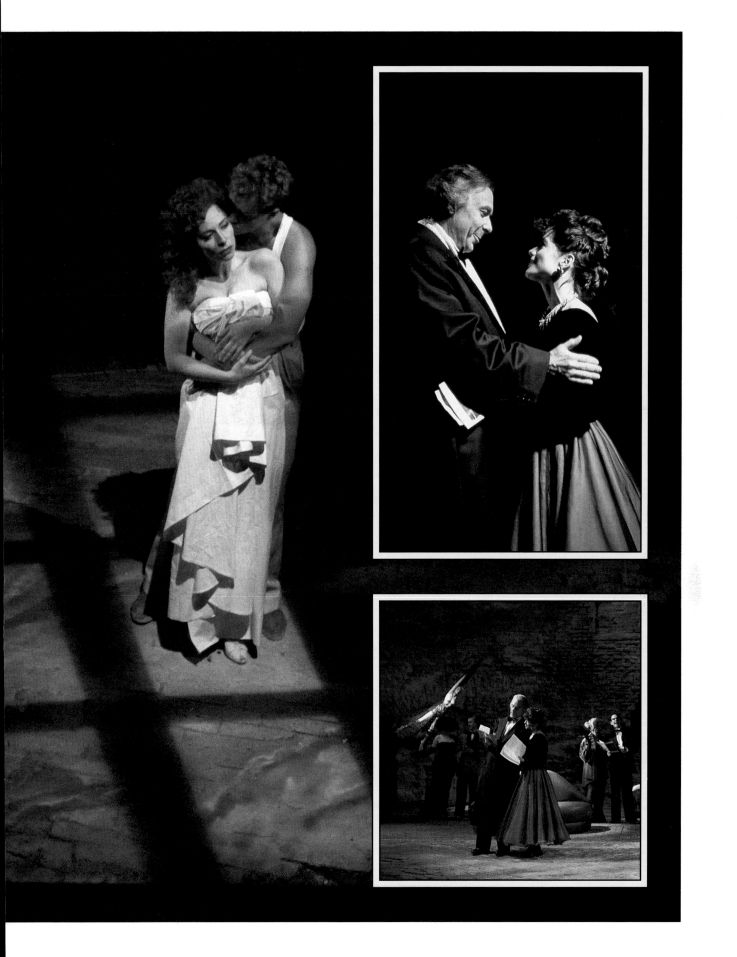

'You must forgive this rude intrusion . . .'
The idyll is broken by George's arrival (*above*)

A gown from an unforgotten past (*left*)

Alone in George's long unused house
(*opposite*)

The gown from the past and the girl from the present remind George of his first wife (*above*)

A secret shared and a sympathy born (*right*)

The mountains at Pau. 'Pas de tendresse et pas de joie, loin d'ici, loin de toi . . .' (*left*)

At the fairground. 'Everybody loves a hero . . .' (*below*)

Overleaf:

Alex meets his uncle's mistress (*top left*)

'God, what a fool I was to love you . . .' (*main picture*)

'She'd be far better off with you . . .' (*top right*)

Giulietta Trapani,
sculptress (*right*)

George's tryst with
Giulietta in Venice is
interrupted by Rose
(*opposite*)

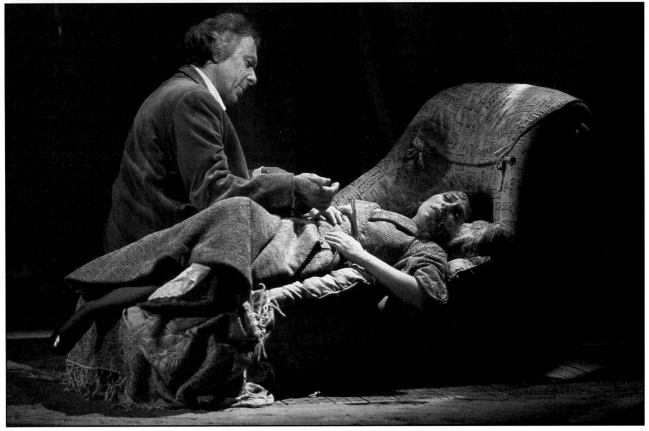

At the wedding of
George and Rose,
Giulietta claims the
best man's kiss
(*above left*)

'My shining leading
lady . . .' (Rose and
Marcel) (*above right*)

'Well done, darling
. . .' Rose Vibert,
now a star, receives
friends in her
dressing-room
(*right*)

After an absence of thirteen years Alex visits Rose in her dressing room, and for the moment Hugo takes a back seat (*above*)

Rose with an autograph hunter (*left*)

A family lunch (*above*)

'I am a mermaid with golden hair . . .' (*left*)

At Pau George now devotes his days to bringing up their daughter, Jenny (*opposite*)

A new friendship blossoms as Jenny grows up (*opposite*)

'I want to be the first man you remember . . .' Jenny's first dance with her father (*left*)

Overleaf:

'Now that's what I call a wall . . .' The happy camaraderie among the estate workers barely masks the tension developing within the family (*main picture*)

'Since you came she's truly blossomed – but, my friend, a flower is fragile . . . Heaven help you if you hurt her . . .' (*top left*)

'Don't let him take her from me . . .' Jealousy in the heart of a man who has always laughed at the word (*top right*)

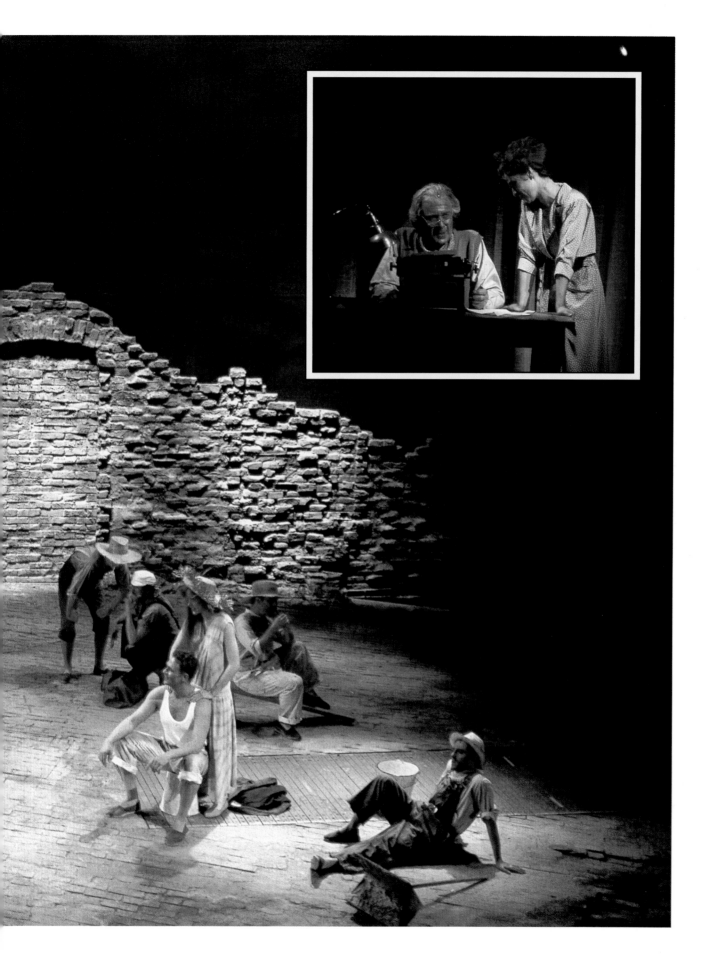

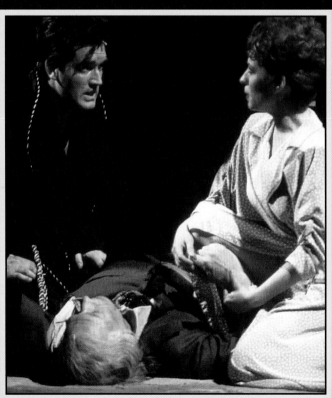

Pages 100 and 101:

'If you reach for the moon ...' A visit to the circus (*main picture*)

'Take the journey of a lifetime ...' (*top left*)

'We are just cousins, Jenny' (*top right*)

George falls – a victim of his own jealousy (*bottom right*)

Preceding pages:

'He asked that everyone should drink his wine, that there should be music and dancing ...'

'Hand me the wine and the dice ...' Giulietta Trapani sings the eulogy of a kindred spirit (*main picture*)

'George would have been so proud of you . . .' Marcel comforts the grieving Rose (*opposite*)

Mother and daughter weep for love that is lost (*left*)

'Anything but lonely . . .' As Alex prepares to leave, both women beg him to stay.

'Love will never, never let you be the same again!' (*left*)

Designs on the Fifties

The time-scale of the novel *Aspects of Love* was always a rather nebulous one. The episode at Pau which sets everything in motion is offhandedly dated by the author in the late 1940s and, as a result, the twenty years of action which are contained in the book take it well into the 1960s – an odd thing for a work which was written in 1955.

Real dating is, of course, something which has very little to do with *Aspects of Love*. It is set in two decades of a glorious 'anytime' which bear little relation to the actual decades of the real world – fine for Garnett and for the printed page, but something which presented a little more difficulty for authors and director trying to bring the tale into some sort of relationship with the real world and to give it a time focus on the stage.

Trevor Nunn and the authors of the musical battled for a considerable time with the twenty-year problem which the author had set them. Basically, the Second World War kept getting in the way. Since the novel made absolutely no reference to the war, it was clearly impossible to have the action straddling the years 1939–45, yet any stretch of twenty years before or after the war bumped into clearly distinguishable periods – the twenties and the sixties – which were at odds with the very flavour of the story, its characters and its action.

At one point Nunn mooted a plan by which the war might be placed in the interval between the acts but, ultimately – and partly because Lloyd Webber had already completed work on some definitely post-war music for one of the earliest scenes – it was decided to stick with the book's starting date in the late 1940s and to run the action on into a sort of never-ending 1950s.

The contributor most affected by this decision was, of course, the designer. Even 'nevertime' has to be placed somewhere in real time for a designer to get a coherent fix on costume design, for the clothes worn by its characters are an important, if often subliminal, element in placing the action of a stage play in its period. Scenery does not necessarily do this – fields and forests are simply fields and forests, and buildings last for centuries without changing their looks, but fashion and clothes can instantly set a show or a scene within a year or two.

From the costuming point of view, Maria Bjørnson was pleased to be fixed in this elongated 1950s period. It was a time of great elegance in clothes, she insisted. The 1950s in France represented the great decade of Dior, Chanel and Balenciaga in clothes, of Picasso, Braque and Modigliani in art. It was a time in which she was happy to linger, and linger, and linger ... as long as she did not have to venture too far into the horrors of the early 1960s, 'the ugliest period of fashion in history'.

With the period of the piece fixed, she set about designing the show's huge repertoire of costumes in an unusual way. For the people of *Aspects of Love* were not, like those of *The Phantom of the Opera*, colourfully romantic characters for whom flamboyant costumes had to be designed, but simply people for whom clothes had to be made. There was a very definite difference.

Delving into endless piles of 1950s' magazines and books – not just fashion catalogues and articles but general picture papers of all kinds, and books and revues devoted to a whole variety of topics and all types of people – Maria and costume supervisor Sue Wilmington began clipping and copying vast quantities of photographs of 1950s' folk and the clothes they wore. Each picture which was chosen went into a folder under the name of a character – this one could be Rose, that one could be Giulietta or Jenny or George or Marcel. And so the piles and the folders grew and grew, filled with ideas and with pictures from which the 'wardrobes' of the *Aspects* people might be compiled.

It was no small task; not merely a matter of finding and making-up one set of clothes per person. The forty to fifty scenes of which the musical was composed at various stages of its development all moved forward inexorably in time, often by significant amounts. There was rarely any likelihood of anyone appearing in the same clothes for two scenes in succession. Rose, for example, needed to be equipped with something approaching twenty-five different outfits. Twenty years' worth of clothes. There would be no question of even the shortest breather for the actress playing Rose during the course of the show. Almost every time she was off-stage, she would have to be changing into a different dress.

Thus, instead of the costume designer confronting the director with a ream of minutely hand-drawn and finished designs – goodness knows how many of which would, in time-honoured fashion, end up being rejected, altered or simply cut as the show was remoulded on its way to the first night – Nunn was met by an artist armed with a vast selection of alternative possibilities for each costume that was needed. Together, they leafed through the pictures, building up sets of clothes, creating the wardrobe each person would wear. Only when that work was done did Maria bring out her pens to begin making the line drawings, over the top of the original photographs and photocopies, which would develop those period dresses into practical stage-wear. In *Aspects of Love* the actors would wear not costumes designed to look like genuine clothes, but genuine clothes adapted and remade as stage costumes.

And that is just what they do.

A quick change
in Act Two.
Geoffrey Abbott's
transformation from
clown to guest at
George's funeral
takes only fifty
seconds

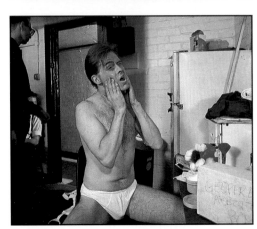

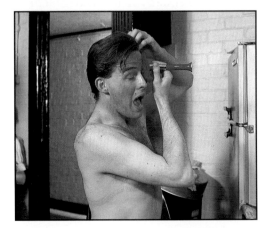

Setting the Scene

Theatre-goers of the 1980s have come to take the considerable wonders of theatrical scenery and mechanics very much – indeed, perhaps too much – for granted. As the successive scenes of a modern show slip swiftly and silently into place, changing from one full stage picture to another, sometimes in a matter of seconds, we are inclined to forget that not so many years ago things were done in a very different way and with a very different effect.

Do you remember the days when a basic stage set consisted of a painted backcloth, cut-out borders and movable wings? If the setting included anything in the way of a solidly built construction, then it had to remain on the stage for the entire act and, while the audience repaired to the bars, sixteen or sixty sweating stagehands bundled it off into the wings and replaced it with the equally hefty second-act scenery. Many a musical show designed, like the majority of plays, in this style was necessarily restricted to one set per act.

Others, whose more wide-ranging plots or demands for a varied stage spectacle necessitated more frequent changes of setting, were constructed on the front-cloth principle. After a scene had been played on the full stage, a painted curtain was dropped and a smaller scene played on the front few feet of the stage while the stage-staff beavered away behind the cloth – all too often audibly cursing and crashing about – to set up the next full-stage scene. This style has survived, crashes, curses and all, mainly in Christmas pantomimes, but only half a dozen years ago it was still to be seen on the West End stage.

Then there was the revolving stage. That eternal, lumbering revolve, originally the province of the melodrama theatres with their picturesque and dramatic series of colourful settings, but introduced into the musical theatre in the 1880s at, of all venues, the little Comedy Theatre, and used endlessly by designers of spectacular and multi-set shows ever since. Like every other style of entertainment and staging, it ultimately became over-used and the sets of some large-scale shows of the 1960s and 1970s seemed never to stop whirling, round and round like a demented ballerina, until the audience could be excused for feeling dizzy just watching the incessant and unvarying motion of the scenery.

The all-purpose set, an unchanging and often bare skeleton

Poster used in *Aspects of Love* Act One,
Scene 3

of a construction which the audience was required to clothe with its own imagination through the various scenes of the show, had its moment of being considered the 'in' thing, but by and large the musical theatre audience has always loved beautiful, picturesque and/or extravagant scenery, and has never been slow in lavishing its applause on the splendid and ingenious mechanical tricks employed by designers and mechanists in set changes or special effects.

In the nineteenth century, the dashingly billed 'spectacular' scenery and effects were impressively described in theatre reports of the day. They would, in spite of their ingenuity, undoubtedly seem tame and artificial to us nowadays, but the importance of the pictorial element of these Victorian musical productions, often three or four hours long and including vast series of sets and costumes, was thoroughly recognized. The scenic designer and mechanist were sometimes credited more prominently on the playbill than the author and composer of the show, and the costumiers, property-makers and special effects designers also featured strongly in the billing. In recent decades, however, the entire physical production and the design element of a show have become more and more intimately tied in with the authors' concepts and the shaping of the show's text.

Modern theatre designers are no longer simply artists. They have to work with engineers, physicists and electronics experts as well. Backstage, a visitor no longer looks at the rows and rows of hemp ropes which were a feature of the wings of a 1950s' theatre, lined up to haul cloths and other pieces of scenery up and down from the parallel pattern of lines suspended in the flies above. Similarly, the series of manually operated, crank-handled winches of the 1960s, ready to haul on to the stage trucks bearing sections of scenery which could not go up and down are gone today; and the stage-manager's corner no longer houses the simple wooden desk of old, equipped with its prompt book and the intercom by which he cues the scene changes, the lighting and the sound. For a major modern show, the corner is now a mass of computer screens and keyboards. The up-to-date theatre of the 1990s – for that is where we are – works by computer. Computers may sound less romantic than the image of a mêlée of muscle-bound men heaving on ropes and cranking on winches in an atmosphere ripe with the smell of greasepaint but, just as the replacement of greasepaint by less messy and more effective modern make-up has been a great step forward for the actor, so the advent of increased mechanization and the computer has allowed designers a scenic richness which could not otherwise have been achieved.

London's Prince of Wales Theatre provides a good example. It was built in 1937, on the site of an earlier theatre of the same name which had housed many famous musicals of the late nineteenth and early twentieth century, and it was, quite naturally, built to suit the scenic conventions of the 1930s. Flats, drops and curtains could go up and down from the flies quite merrily, but it was not thought necessary to allow for anything of size or importance to come in and out from the wings.

No one bothered much about this, for it was a layout which suited perfectly the plays and revues which filled the theatre for the first twenty years of its existence and, when musicals finally became the preferred fare at the Prince of Wales, their designers simply had to stick to the old-fashioned styles of design which the stage, with its very narrow wing-space, allowed them. Often these shows had toured or played a season in the provinces prior to finding a home in the West End and their scenic content was limited enough for them to close an out-of-town week on a Saturday and open in London the following week, after a traditionally hectic 'get in' over the weekend.

Aspects of Love, with its varied scenic plot and the almost cinematic swiftness of some of its sections, simply could not have been staged under these old-fashioned conditions as its writers and director envisaged it. The fluidity and speed of the most sophisticated mechanical scenic methods were vital to the piece. The talents of the show's designer, Maria Bjørnson, and the breadth of her technical as well as artistic knowledge were set a fine problem: how to illustrate both the helter-skelter action of the show's early stages and the more leisurely scenes of the second act – the many and varied indoor scenes on the one hand, and the mighty grace of the Pyrenees and the expansive, autumnal ease of the French farmyard on the other – on a stage space laid out for the design methods of another age?

The plan which Miss Bjørnson evolved looks quite straightforward and natural as, sitting in the theatre, you watch the gloriously atmospheric scenes of *Aspects of Love* slide effortlessly past. So it should. That is its art. But that apparent effortlessness covers many complex elements of scenic and mechanical design which just could not have been envisaged even a few years earlier.

Only the finely calculated aid of powerful motorization and computerization can allow, for example, the dazzling effect produced when the back wall of the set splits into two jagged halves, the top portion rising to exactly the right height to display the mountains behind it and then closing again to hang suspended, at precisely one metre above its matching half, before ending its journey the merest fraction away from its partner. The top half must not actually meet the lower half, as the shock and the grating noise of the meeting and separating of the two weighty pieces would be dreadful. The computer ensures that the pieces are stopped dead at the right point, but in the audience one is none the wiser. There is no noise, no shaking scenery and, because there is nothing to see or hear, one simply does not think about it. But the designer and her production manager had to. Those two huge pieces of scenery had to be constructed to the millimetre, the lower half installed on the stage and the upper hung above it with equally minute care, and the motors connected to both the scenery and to the

Poster for Act Two, Scene 2

119

computer controlling it adjusted to a feather's touch of exactitude.

Clearly a show of such mechanical complexities was not to be easily conceived, built in a cheerfully approximate way and installed in its theatre in a hurried weekend, in the manner of the pre-war Prince of Wales Theatre pieces. It was not. The 'get-in' time for *Aspects of Love* was counted in months rather than days, as areas of the available space around the stage were reorganized and even rebuilt to house the workings of the show.

It was three months ahead of the scheduled April opening date that the Prince of Wales Theatre was handed over to the show's production office, Martyn Hayes Associates, to oversee the 'get-in'. The previous show had closed on the Saturday, and on Monday 16 January 1989 the first steps towards the manufacture of *Aspects of Love* were taken.

It was not, by any stretch of the imagination, a case of starting to bring anything in. Not for a long time. Before even the tiniest bit of the scenery of the show could be brought into the theatre, a whole lot of what was already there had to be taken out. It was a case of stripping the whole theatre down to the buff; a case of starting from the very basics, practically from the theatre walls themselves, and building everything up from there. For the first and most obvious problem facing the scenic team was one of space. Not just space for storage of the scenery and properties for what was a substantial scenic show in the tiny wings, but space on the stage itself.

The Prince of Wales Theatre stage is shaped like a lopsided oblong. It has a proscenium opening of 12.8 metres and a height of 6.86 metres . . . so far, so good. But from the footlights to the back wall it offers a depth of only 7.5 metres, more or less. More or less, because that back wall is far from straight. It follows the shape of the theatre building, constructed to fill an irregularly shaped site and slanting outwards as it makes its way up the hillside towards Coventry Street. A shallow stage with a slanting back: two disadvantages which had either to be made into advantages or else eliminated.

There was little choice as regards the depth. Somehow it had to be increased. That meant either burrowing through the back wall on to the street or pushing forward into the auditorium. The one option was almost as bad as the other, for if to burrow backwards was structurally and practically impossible, as well as trespassing on the public highway, to push forward would create a potential problem with the sound department of Martin Levan, if the pit was covered, and/or involve losing some of the auditorium and with it rows of seats which were vital in balancing the books of the show. Every seat lost would represent nearly £10,000 per annum in lost revenue, and when you start counting up the resultant cost of a row, the big red figures become very alarming very quickly.

But to come forward was the only answer, so a plan had to be devised which would not eat up too much of the auditorium. It was decided that, in effect, just over a metre extra would be

The set is built just centimetres from the theatre's outer wall

sufficient. The orchestra pit could be moved forward and the space which it had previously occupied covered by a vast over-hanging false stage under which the orchestra members could be housed. And so, as the various teams moved into the Prince of Wales to begin to strip out not only the stage area itself but the entire auditorium, the lighting grid, the flies, the perch above the stage from where the lighting operation was carried out, and any other space which might render up useful square metres, the first positive step was made. A space just over a metre wide was hacked from the auditorium to make space for the extended orchestra pit.

Bit by bit, the naked theatre underwent the various oper-ations needed to get it into *Aspects of Love* working order. While the stage space was being prepared, the whole auditorium underwent a facelift and redecoration, the entire backstage wir-ing system was pulled out and the lines which were to hold the extensive electrical input which the show's machinery required were replaced with fresh wiring. The theatre's lighting board was pulled out from the lighting gallery and sent off to be over-hauled, and by the time it returned its old home was no longer available, for the prompt corner, traditionally housed along-side the proscenium arch on the left-hand side of the stage, had moved in. It had, in fact, simply gone upwards. Instead of occu-pying its usual place at stage level, it had been raised three metres to what had been the lighting gallery, and there, hover-ing above the stage, the stage-manager and his team of staff with their various computerized boards and screens were to be installed.

Andrew Bridge, the lighting designer, and his lighting department were given a new base in what had been the theatre's projection box. In less happy days, the Prince of Wales had earned its owners a few extra pounds by doubling as a cinema showing Chinese films, and a projection box had been installed at the back of the Dress Circle. With its global view of the full stage and auditorium, it was an ideal place in which to headquarter the operators in charge of the barrage of stage lights. The sound desk, alone, held its now customary place at the back of the stalls, but the stripping down of the theatre al-lowed the principal speakers of the sound system to be built into the redesigned and rebuilt proscenium arch, instead of tower-ing in ugly heaps in front of the period décor.

The planning and building of the actual stage area itself was a long and complex job, for it involved, in effect, the build-ing of an entire new false stage on top of the existing one, not only in order to gain the additional space by its overhang but also to house, in the cavity between the old and new stages, the mass of machinery which would be required to operate the various sections of scenery.

The elements which make up the setting of *Aspects of Love* fall basically, like those of any other show, into two groups, those which go up and down and those which go from side to side. Or, to put it more theatrically, those which are flown and

Andrew Bridge

those which are stacked and moved at stage level. These two groups combine to gain the maximum in the way of both pictorial effectiveness and fluidity and, to achieve that maximum, considerable imagination and mechanical ingenuity are required.

At the basis of the set of the show is what is called the 'back wall'. It is not actually the back wall of the theatre, even though it may look like it. It is the vast stone-painted piece, already spoken of, which fills the back of the stage and which splits so dramatically to produce effects such as the mountainous Pyrenean scene and the passionately red background for the wake sequence. In front of that wall are hung, on the grid of narrowly spaced lines, the other principal pieces of large scenery – the French house with its trees, the tilted back wall of Giulietta's studio, George's Paris apartment with its see-through wall of paintings, the various sets of drapes, the station scene, the theatre alley – each, like the back wall, linked to the computers which set in motion the motors which raise and lower them and which ensure that they stop dead precisely at the level of the stage.

It is, however, at stage level that ingenuity has really had to be exercised and where it has been combined with modern technology to such an extent that the potential handicap of the theatre's tiny wing space has been entirely overcome. Miss Bjørnson devised a set of eight tall, slatted screens, stretching the full height of the proscenium arch, from the floor to the flies. These screens (which have become known affectionately to the company – in the show's absence of a line of dancing girls – as Ada, Betty, Cissie, Doris, Ethel, Fifi, Gertrude and Hannah) are attached to tracks above, which allow them to run from side to side across the stage in two very close, parallel lines, but each is also equipped with an individual motor by which it can be turned through a full 360 degrees. Thus the separate units can be formed up in a straight line, filling the whole of the stage opening with what looks like a vast panel of slatted shutters, or placed in a variety of angled combinations and patterns in which they represent such settings as the wings of the theatres in Montpellier and Paris in the opening scenes of the two acts, and all the various rooms of the house in Pau in quick succession.

They can be set in action singly, in small groups, or all at once, as they waltz cleanly and quickly across the stage under the silent power of their motors to the pre-set positions stored in the brain of their own particular computer. And when they are not needed, instead of having to be carted or dragged off into the wings like old-fashioned scenery, they spin dutifully into a line, like a crocodile of well-behaved schoolgirls, and shuffle sweetly to the side of the stage to stack themselves up in a compact pile, at right-angles to the footlights, where they await the call of their computer to glide once more into action.

Combined with the flown pieces, the family of screens supplies the major part of the scenic design, but they have to be

The stage is set:
George's Paris flat
(*left*); the house at
Pau (*below*)

The furniture and properties are stored in the wings with space-saving exactitude, ready to be moved by stage crew and travellator to set up scenes such as the art gallery (*below*)

Some props, like the spring-loaded painting (*left*), have an active job to do. Others, like the desks (*below*), have a dual purpose. These double as make-up tables in the theatre scenes and as café tables shortly afterwards

complemented by the various set furnishings – the tables and chairs, the beds and the statues – which cannot be flown (although someone will probably one day invent a computerized capsule which lowers or raises an entire stageful of furnishings in one go) but need to be shunted in from the wings. The days when all these pieces were carried on are long gone and the days when they were winched on via movable rostra or 'trucks' must now be on the way out. In this instance almost everything is moved on and off the stage on a set of wooden 'travelators'. These stout, multi-slatted rolling carpets, set into the stage surface, stretch from the wings to the centre of the stage. The furniture, stored until needed in a tightly constructed and ordered heap, is set on the portion hidden in the wings and moved on stage on cue by the touch of a computerized button which sets the travelators rolling into their pre-set position. It is still just possible for a carelessly set piece to tumble from its travelator, but the carpets are much smoother than the dangerously lurching old truck system, as well as being infinitely swifter and more silent.

The ingenuity of the set does not stop there. The stage's top surface holds, for example, several trapdoors. The functions of some are obvious enough – one represents the trapdoor in the hayloft in the second act, for example – but others are less so. From one of these unseen apertures all of the circus bleachers arise, unfolding from a compact concertina of metal into the large piece of scenery which we see, and which can hold almost all the principal cast at once without rocking. Another tiny little trapdoor at the front of the stage allows the swift and unnoticed setting of the single shoe, which Alex mysteriously discovers at the house at Pau on the night Rose has worn the famous dress. So many items, large and small, all of which had to be thought of before the first nail went into the stage.

That process – the building of the new stage – was, naturally, one of the first steps forward. It began with a vast delivery of steel girders. These great metal pieces were knitted together across the whole surface of the stage to form the framework on which the new surface could be constructed. Into this skeleton of steel, raking downwards from the back of the stage and over the edge of the orchestra pit, were installed the steel frames which would support the moving travelators, the outlines of the trapdoors, and the positions which would hold the various motors. On to the rear of that skeleton, the two-part back wall was erected. And, saving every square centimetre of stage space, it was erected not parallel to the stage front, but following the angle of the theatre's outer wall.

While the steel stage skeleton was being fabricated, a very much larger amount of steel was going into another part of the theatre – the ceiling void above the stage. Something like eight or nine tons of reinforcing material was hoisted into that empty roof space, which probably had not had a visitor – and certainly not a great girder through it – since its original construction. That vast metal bulk had an extremely practical purpose. It was to hold everything up. The amount of flown scenery in *Aspects of Love* was not only so huge as to raise questions about whether enough lines could be squeezed in to hold it all, but it was of a weight which, without such reinforcement, was perfectly capable of bringing the theatre roof in.

The most monumental piece to be flown was, of course, the upper half of the back wall and, common sense *oblige*, it was the first piece of scenery as such to be brought into the theatre. Hoisted on six lines, with trusses to guide its movement, the huge and heavy piece was manœuvred into place and connected up to the motor which would drive it, which was itself installed under the framework of the new stage. The bottom half followed. Brought to the theatre in a series of rough-cut panels, it was built on to the stage where, once it was in position, it could be both made to fit precisely with its other half and, subsequently, textured and painted and blended with the stage surface.

The travelators and their motors were next to be installed. It had been decided to construct these important pieces from wood rather than use a continuous rubberized belt, as wood provided a more solid support for the furniture they would have to carry. But the work involved in producing the long wooden, slatted mats was vast. Each piece was built on to two chains – one at each running side – on to which each slat had to be individually bolted with not one but four separate bolts. By the time some 650 slats and more than 2,500 bolts had been laboriously and carefully secured in place, there was at least one workman in the Prince of Wales Theatre who was wishing that the rubber belt had been chosen. Only when all these individual pieces of stage machinery, jigsawed into their proper places, had been installed, could the stage be fully covered in.

If there was a jigsaw down below, however, up above things were having to be worked out to the millimetre. The shallowness of the stage meant, naturally, that the flies held room for only a limited number of lines, and every line – each of which meant another piece of scenery – which could possibly be crammed into the practicable working space was crammed in. It was not easy. Some scenic ideas simply had to be abandoned, others modified. The atmospheric fingers of the tree-branches growing over the garden in Pau had to be pruned quite severely when they threatened to catch in the scenery hanging from the nearest line. For 'nearest' was only a centimetre or two away.

One by one, the various items to be flown arrived at the theatre. Built in the scenery workshops, the largest of them then had to be sawn into pieces to allow them to fit through the doors into the theatre, and re-welded together once they had been put into place. However, the tightly and intricately constructed mass of pieces suspended in the flies, even when they all slid smoothly past each other without a hitch, produced another problem for another department. What was to be done about Andrew Bridge's lighting equipment which needed, equally, to be above the stage? There quite simply was not room for it.

Settings: the Pyrenean mountain range, the café in Montpellier, and the sun-stained branches of the Béarnais trees

127

Even though the lights here are less obvious than in most theatres, there is an enormous battery of lamps positioned in all corners of the stage and theatre, to produce the uncountable number of small and subtle variations of light as well as the large, obvious effects which appear in the course of *Aspects of Love*. How and where could all these lights be placed when the normal position for many of them was filled up by scenery? The answer could not have been more logical. If the stage could be extended forward, why not the flies as well? An overhanging stage could be echoed by an overhanging proscenium.

Thus a great, overhanging pelmet, textured and painted to carry on unobtrusively the stonework pattern of the stage scenery, was designed and constructed, reaching out from the upper transversal of the proscenium arch and dissimulating under its cornice the necessary bars of lights. This set of lights was supplemented by another series situated on a custom-built walkway suspended from the theatre roof, way above the stalls, which replaced the more common batteries which disfigure the Dress Circle frontage of many theatres.

Elsewhere, lamps nestled in every available nook and cranny of the stage, with some lighting bars even constructed specially to interlock with the bars supporting the flown scenery. The area between the 'back wall' and the actual theatre wall is the most remarkable of all. In little more than a metre of space are housed more lamps than you would believe possible. To stand there and look upwards is to look into a sea of little light bulbs of all kinds and colours, layered between the outer wall and the profiled mountains, between the mountains and the gauze cloth which separates them from the main 'back wall', and so forth, and even attached to the back of the moving portion of the wall.

Four hundred lamps. But even this was not enough. There simply was not enough space in the right places to affix lamps which could do the work that was needed. What was the way around such a problem? Once again mechanics provided the answer. If there was no place to put a lamp where it could shine at a certain time with a certain coloured gel on a certain spot, then one of the lamps for which there was space would have to do the job instead. How? Quite simply it would have to move. And, when necessary, change its own focus and/or its own gel and . . .

This was clearly a problem for a real expert, and a real expert, in the person of a university professor, was duly put to work to develop a light which could do practically everything but think for itself. The result was PALS – the Precision Automated Lighting System, an amazing little creature which fulfilled all requirements. PALS are almost frighteningly alive. Each lamp, set on a pivot, is equipped with five small, personal motors which allows it to turn its 'head' around like a sunflower chasing the sun, panning and/or tilting as required to line itself up on its objective. One of its motors allows it to change its own gel, another to refocus as required. If there was a lamps' union,

Stage lighting: some of the lights used to give the audience a wing-side view of the Montpellier stage (*left*). Close-up of a screen motor and its operator (*top*); a motorized zip frame (*above*)

they would undoubtedly go on strike, for each PALS does the work of innumerable of its brethren. But Andrew Bridge's lighting plot still needed no less than thirty of them.

The PALS, however, are only one element in the mechanical skein which supports the visual side of the show. The others are largely those which combine, with the aid of nearly fifty motors, to operate the various scenic changes.

The computers and buttons and the vast cupboard full of electric and electronic material which set in motion all this intricate square dance of scenic action are housed in the dark recesses of the five-by-two-metre 'tree house' constructed in the old lighting gallery. Up the little iron ladder, behind the board where the stage-manager is perched orchestrating the running of the show, the three-man team which operates the scenic movement of the piece has its home. The chief console operator has, at his fingertips, a pair of what look just like word-processor keyboards, and in front of him a pair of vibrantly busy screens which flicker and bounce with multi-coloured information.

The one on the right is all about Ada and Betty and Cissie and Co., and you can see them there, on the screen. Eight little brown stripes, lined up on a baby blue background, in a straight and soldierly line, ready to start the show. Above them, a panel of figures lists the current position of each — how far across the stage it is and at what angle on its axis. When the opening song has ended, the first cue is entered on the keyboard and . . . go! The waltz of the screens begins. First Ada, Betty and Cissie take a ninety-degree turn. The figures flash round like a fruit machine and, as the scenery moves, the three brown lines which represent the three furthest screens replace themselves in the new pattern on the monitor.

In goes another cue and off they go again, shuffling prettily about to form themselves into a grouping which represents the dressing-rooms of the Montpellier Theatre, and before long they are on the move yet again, twirling their way towards the wings to take their first rest-break. They will not be needed for a few more minutes, until they are required to line up behind a large gauze curtain and represent the walls and windows of George's villa at Pau. George's villa is the big moment in this department, for the other screen and keyboard at this station look after the gauze curtain. Since it has to come in marginally after, but very definitely after, the seven screens have tiptoed across into position, in order to avoid a giant gauze tangle, it was logical to have it operated in tandem. So this time both screens flash in turn and, while the audience sees only what looks like a simple bit of scene-changing, there is a rainbow of action going on in the darkness above the stage.

In between these bursts of screenic activity, things have not been idle in the corner where the other two operators sit. Their board might not be as entertaining to look at, but it is equally important. There is no technicolour screen in this corner, just a staunch grey board equipped with large, practical-looking

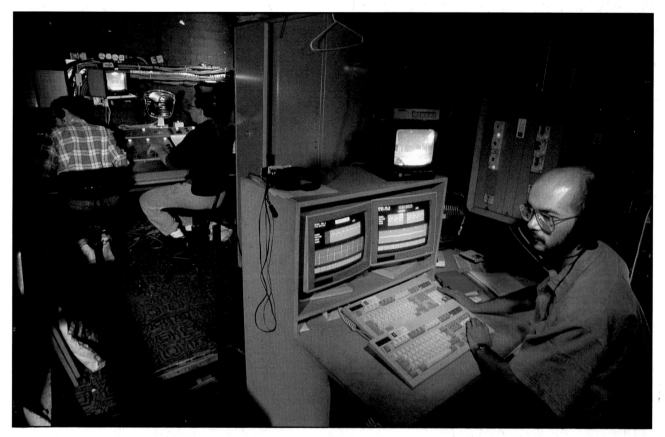

switches and big green off–on lights, and a lot of flashing red numbers which turn out to be very relevant. The first two portions of the panel operate the two travelators, the third operates the back wall and the fourth the important door panel on the far side of the stage which has to be opened to let the sometimes bulky contents of the travelator through on to the stage.

The operator punches out a set of figures on a panel-within-a-panel that resembles a calculator or a press-button telephone and the red lights flash up the result. He has keyed in the next position of the travelator or of the wall and, when the cue comes, he simply has to hit the 'activate' button and the computer does the rest while he busily resets the panel for the next cue. There are some moments when things hot up remarkably, and it is not difficult to see why the board needs to be manned by two people when panels five, six, seven, eight, nine or ten call for attention to fly in various pieces of scenery just when both the travelators need to be set rolling at the same time. And just in case a piece of gauze or a tree branch gets caught up in something it should not get caught up in, there is a large and comforting red stop button in the middle of the panel.

It is rather like a mini-bunker, this centre of operations. Something out of a James Bond film. You get a glimpse of the stage when the screens are spread out across the floor, but otherwise the only real contact with the outside world is via a handful of monitors connected to the closed-circuit cameras which are trained on the show. The stage-manager also has one pointed at the conductor, which means he has a view of the

Screens: a console operator, perched above the stage, watches the dance of the scenery on his multi-coloured screens

The *Aspects of Love*
chorus line of screens
lines up to form the
windows of the house
at Pau. Behind them,
the actors prepare
their entrance

ankles and, if he is very lucky, of the knees of any young women
who happen to be sitting in the middle of row A – a bright
moment for a fellow who is stuck in the dark pounding his way
through a vast and complicated list of cues for three hours a day
and six on matinées, making sure that everything that is supposed to happen in the show actually does happen when and as
it ought to.

Motors and computers may mean that there is less purely
physical effort needed in the scenic running of a show, and that
the backstage operation is nowadays undertaken by a differently trained group of men and women, but their workload is
still a mighty one. There are only a couple of times in the course
of the show when any one of the operators can slip down the
ladder and out into the alley for a breath of fresh air. Most of the
time they have to be continually on the *qui vive* as the evening's
action unfolds, possibly just a tiny bit differently from the night
before. But the mechanization of the show does mean that such
variations are very small.

Systems like that evolved for *Aspects of Love* have meant a
vast gain in reliability, accuracy and safety. Like their human
counterparts, the *Aspects of Love* chorus line of Ada, Betty and
Cissie has been known to suffer the mechanical equivalent of a
twisted ankle in the middle of a performance – no one, not even
a computerized screen, is wholly stage-perfect – but by and
large they make up an impeccable team with the boys in the
bunker, stylishly sweeping the show along in that smooth series
of scenes which could not have been attempted or even imagined in the theatre not so very long ago.

Libretto

Synopsis of scenes and principal musical numbers

ACT ONE

Prologue:

Railway station at Pau, 1964	Love Changes Everything	*Alex, Giulietta*

France, 1947

A small theatre in Montpellier		*Rose, Marcel, Ensemble*
A café in Montpellier	Parlez-vous français?	*Rose, Alex, Marcel,*
		Crooner, Ensemble
The railway station		*Rose, Alex*
In a train compartment	Seeing is Believing	*Rose, Alex*
The house at Pau		*Rose, Alex*
An art exhibition in Paris	A Memory of a Happy Moment	*George, Giulietta*
In many rooms in the house at Pau		*Rose, Alex*
On the terrace		*Rose, Alex, George*
Outside the bedroom		*Rose, Alex*
Up in the Pyrenees	Chanson d'enfance	*Rose, Alex*
The house at Pau		*Rose, Alex*

Two years pass . . .

A fairground in Paris	Everybody Loves a Hero	*Ensemble, Fairground Barkers, Alex*
	First Orchestral Interlude	*Elizabeth, Alex, Rose*
George's flat in Paris	She'd Be Far Better Off With You	*Alex, George*
	Second Orchestral Interlude	
Giulietta's studio in Venice	Stop, Wait, Please	*Giulietta, George*
A registry office		*Registrar, Rose, George, Giulietta, Marcel, Ensemble*
A military camp in Malaya		*Alex*

ACT TWO

	Orchestral Introduction to Act Two	

Thirteen years later . . .

A theatre in Paris	Leading Lady	*Marcel, Rose, Hugo, Ensemble*
At the stage door		*Rose, Alex*
George's house at Pau	Other Pleasures	*George*
		George, Jenny, Alex, Rose
A café in Venice	There is More to Love	*Giulietta*
The garden at Pau		*George, Rose, Alex, Jenny*
	Mermaid Song	*Jenny, Alex*
The countryside around the house		*Jenny, Alex*
	Third Orchestral Interlude	

Two years pass . . .

The garden at Pau		*George, Rose, Alex, Hugo*
On the terrace	The First Man You Remember	*George, Jenny*
In the vineyard at Pau		*Rose, George, Alex, Jenny, Hugo, Ensemble*
Up in the Pyrenees		*Jenny, Alex*
George's study at Pau		*George, Rose*
A circus in Paris	Journey of a Lifetime	*Chanteuse, Ensemble*
Outside the circus		*George, Rose, Alex, Jenny*
Jenny's bedroom in Paris		*Alex, Jenny, George*
The vineyards at Pau	Hand Me the Wine and the Dice	*Giulietta, Ensemble, Rose*
		Marcel, Hugo, Alex, Jenny
A hay loft		*Alex, Giulietta*
On the terrace		*Jenny, Alex*
	Anything But Lonely	*Rose*
		Alex, Giulietta

Act One

A vertical line indicates areas of the text where there is a substantial overlapping of different voices.

All bold type indicates sung lines.

SCENE 1

(Music. A man discovered on stage, singing to a woman. Only later are we to identify him as the 34-year-old ALEX)

ALEX
Love,
Love changes everything:
Hands and faces,
Earth and sky,
Love,
Love changes everything:
How you live and
How you die.

Love
Can make the summer fly,
Or a night
Seem like a lifetime.

Yes, love,
Love changes everything:
Now I tremble
At your name.
Nothing in the
World will ever
Be the same.

Love,
Love changes everything:
Days are longer,
Words mean more.
Love,
Love changes everything:
Pain is deeper
Than before.

Love
Will turn your world around,
And that world
Will last for ever.

Yes, love,
Love changes everything,
Brings you glory,
Brings you shame.
Nothing in the
World will ever
Be the same.

Why did I go back to see her...?

WOMAN (GIULIETTA)
Alex, it's all in the past...

ALEX
Off
Into the world we go,
Planning futures,
Shaping years.

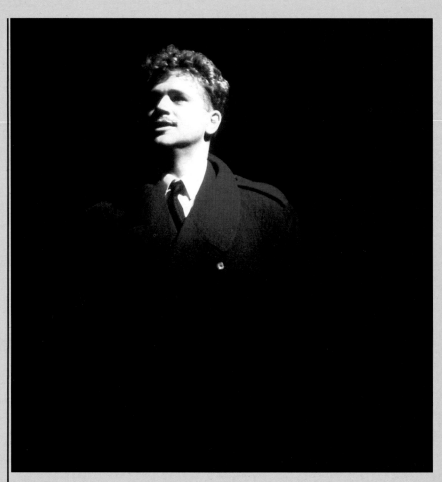

Love
Bursts in, and suddenly
All our wisdom
Disappears.

Love
Makes fools of everyone:
All the rules
We make are broken.

Yes, love,
Love changes everyone.
Live or perish
In its flame.
Love will never,
Never let you
Be the same.

(The number does not finish formally, but cuts into...)

SCENE 2

(A small provincial theatre in Montpellier, France, 1947. View from backstage. The closing lines of a poorly attended performance of Ibsen's The Master Builder, *the last of the season.*

Among the cast are MARCEL, the troupe's actor-manager and ROSE, its 25-year-old leading lady, who plays HILDE WANGEL)

A VOICE *(down in the garden)*
The master builder is dead!

OTHER VOICES *(nearer)*
His head is all smashed in... He fell right into the quarry.

HILDE (ROSE) *(turns to RAGNAR and says quietly)*
I can't see him up there now.

RAGNAR
This is terrible. So in fact he couldn't do it.

HILDE (ROSE) *(with a kind of quiet, bewildered triumph)*
But he got right to the top.

(waves the shawl upwards and shouts with wild intensity)

My... my... master builder!
(Curtain. Limp applause. Curtain call. Curtain falls again. ACTORS and STAGE-HANDS mill about. ROSE rounds furiously on MARCEL)

134

ROSE
The toast of the town?
The hit of the year?
The birth of a star?
The end of a career?

MARCEL
Darling, these things happen ...

ROSE
You turn round and tell us
We're closed for two weeks!

MARCEL
Rose, I thought of everything ...

ROSE
You thought of nothing!

MARCEL
... There are posters in the streets
And banners in the squares.
Scream away, feel free,
But at Ibsen, not at me ...

ROSE (interrupting)
Why did I agree
To accept this bloody tour?
The only thing in store
Is two weeks of nothing!

ACTORS (in the background, to one another)
Win some, lose some ...
What the hell ...

ROSE
Working till I drop
For an audience of four:
Three nuns and your mother ...

MARCEL
It's no good complaining ...

ROSE
And she only bothered
Because it was raining!

MARCEL
Love ...

ROSE
Don't call me 'Love'!

MARCEL
... This isn't personal.

ACTORS (departing, to one another)
I don't care ...
The theatre's my life ...

MARCEL
We will start the tour again
In Lyon in two weeks!
Rose, the people there
Are all Ibsen mad, I swear!
Come on, show me a smile!

ROSE (turning away)
God, I'm not in the mood ...

MARCEL
What's a fortnight or so?

ROSE
With no money or food ...

MARCEL
Don't be glum ...

ROSE
Don't waste your breath ...

ACTORS
Don't let's be downhearted!
We'll get by ...

(Dodging the issue, MARCEL beckons forward the
17-year-old ALEX, who has been lurking in the
background)

MARCEL
Now Rose, you must meet this young man!
He's a dedicated fan —
Been in every evening!

ROSE
Marcel, don't run away —
I can see your little plan.

ALEX (approaching nervously)
It's an honour, mam'selle,
I could watch you for hours ...
You can't have forgotten,
I threw you the flowers ...
Mam'selle, seeing you on stage
Has changed my life!

ACTORS (exiting, to one another and to ROSE)
Join us in the café
In the square!

ROSE
See you ...
The café ...
The square ...

ALEX (to ROSE, tentatively)
Would you let
Me walk you there ...?

(Dissolve to ...)

135

SCENE 3

(A café in Montpellier. Later the same evening. MARCEL, MEMBERS OF THE TROUPE, WAITERS. ROSE and ALEX in the forefront, alone at a table. A CROONER sings on a wireless playing in the background which is tuned into the American Forces Network. ACTORS are occasionally heard chatting)

CROONER
'Parlez-vous
français?
Je suis sad.
Parlez-vous
français?
I feel bad.

How do you say
'Ce soir vous êtes si
belle'?

I only know
A word or so,
Like 'Cat' and
'School' —
Je suis fool.

ACTOR 1 *(to COMPANIONS)*
Death to him
Who dares mention Ibsen!

ALEX *(to ROSE)*
One day Montpellier's
Going to scream...

*Parlez-vous
français?*

ACTOR 2
Death to all directors!

Please say 'oui'.

ALEX *(continuing)*
... To get you back!
Shall I order?
An espresso?
Or cappuccino?

*Parlez-vous
français?
Speak to me.*

ROSE *(flatly)*
Armagnac.

How do you say:

ACTOR 3
Why we bothered heaven knows.

'Vous êtes jolie,

ACTOR 4
Marcel's a dreamer.

ACTOR 1
Marcel deserves
The firing squad.

Mam'sell'?

ALEX *(to WAITER)*
Armagnac.
And a glass of house white for me.

ACTOR 2 *(looking across at ROSE)*
Who's she with?

(The OTHERS shrug. One of the other ACTORS, exiting, takes his leave of ROSE)

ACTOR 5
Two weeks
Before we meet again.

Chérie,

ROSE *(unsmiling)*
Two weeks
Before we eat again.

*Where do I
commencer,
f you won't parler
français with me?*

WAITER *(returning with the ACTORS' bill)*
Is that all?

ACTORS 1, 2 & 3 *(to one another)*
The same again?

ACTOR 4 *(to WAITER)*
The same again.

(The WAITER goes off, crossing with MARCEL who has just arrived. The ACTORS hail him)

ACTORS 1, 2, 3 & 4
Here's the man
Of the hour!

*Parlez-vous
français?*

ROSE *(to ALEX)*
Please promise me
You'll answer...

Say you do.

MARCEL *(to the ACTORS)*
Am I allowed
To join you?

(MARCEL sits down with the ACTORS, who are looking across at ROSE)

ACTORS *(to MARCEL)*
Who's with Rose?

ROSE *(continuing)*
... Truthfully.

ALEX
What's the question?

ROSE
You must promise first.

*Parlez-vous
français?*

ALEX
I promise, I promise.

MARCEL *(replying to the ACTORS)*
Rose's young fan!

Tell me true.

ROSE
How old are you?

How do you say:

ALEX
In three years
I'll be twenty.

'Je suis unhappy

(ACTOR 1, who has sidled up to ROSE, overhears this)

ACTOR 1 *(to ROSE)*
Is this your
Younger brother, Rose?

Fella'?

ROSE *(ignoring the ACTOR, to ALEX)*
Is that all?

ACTOR *(hisses loudly back to the OTHERS)*
Seventeen!

WAITER *(returning to ROSE and ALEX with their drinks)*
Is that all?

(ROSE downs the brandy in one and hands the empty glass back to the WAITER)

ROSE
Another Armagnac.

(The WAITER goes off and ACTOR 1 returns to the OTHERS, highly amused)

ACTORS *(shouting across to ROSE)*
You're in with
A chance there!

*Chérie,
Adieu to drinks
and danser,*

(ROSE ignores them. Other ACTORS are by now beginning to drift out)

*If you won't parler
français
With me.
Unless you say
'oui'...*

ALEX
I have this theory:

If you think
What those images mean,
Then clearly
Most of Ibsen's subtext
Is obscene...

*Adieu to drinks
and danser,
If you won't parler
français
With me.'*

ROSE *(dryly)*
Seventeen...

ALEX
It makes one very aware ... such fearfully
modern ideas ...

(He is interrupted, by MARCEL)

MARCEL *(to ROSE)*
Darling, it's only two weeks ...

*(He blows her a kiss and departs. The CROONER's
song has come to an end. We hear the voice of the
RADIO ANNOUNCER:)*

ANNOUNCER
Johnny Lejeune with 'Parlez-vous français?'
Encore, Johnny!

*(The radio orchestra starts up again and we hear the
opening bars of the song)*

CROONER
'Parlez-vous français?
Je suis sad ...'

ROSE *(calling across to the BARTENDER)*
Oh, turn that thing off!

*(The BARTENDER shrugs and turns off the
wireless. By this time the café is more or less
deserted).*

I don't need some crooner crooning.
Or a stage-door Johnny swooning.
Look, if I'm not very nice to you,
It's because I have things to worry me.
But thanks for the flowers every night ...

(A pause. She explains)

I'm resting again.
That's what actresses say
When they're not in a play.

(Another pause)

You're a long way from England.

ALEX
Yes.

ROSE
And what brings you to Montpellier?

ALEX
I'm travelling through France
Until my call-up.

ROSE
You mean the army?

ALEX
May I ask a stupid question?
How will you survive for two weeks?

ROSE
I'll get along somehow.

ALEX
What, with no money?
May I make a bold suggestion?

ROSE
And what kind of 'bold suggestion'?

ALEX
Come away with me, Rose ...

ROSE
With you? Where?

ALEX
I have a villa —
Don't be suspicious —
You won't believe it,
The view of the Pyrenees!
I leave this evening —
Come with me ...

ROSE *(after a pause)*
Are you sure you want me to accept?

(No reply)

Very well, then,
I accept.

(Still no reply. ALEX is in a daze)

ROSE
Here. Have some Armagnac.

*(He drinks and returns the glass. She too takes a sip,
as if to seal their agreement. Then breaks the moment
with:)*

ROSE
Not another night
In this hateful city!

ALEX
You'll need to pack —
We'll meet at the station.

ROSE
I'll pick up my script and my dress.
By the way ...

ALEX
Yes?

ROSE
... What's your name?
No — let me guess ...
Rupert?

ALEX
No. It's Alex.

ROSE
Alex.
Hello.
I'm Rose.

ALEX
I know.

(They hurry in opposite directions. Dissolve to ...)

SCENE 4

*(Gare de Montpellier. Later the same night. ALEX
waiting anxiously)*

ALEX *(pacing, finally exploding)*
That girl can really act!
I could have sworn that she'd be here!
She's got a great career —
She should play Salomé!
Maybe I was mad,
But she really seemed sincere ...

(ROSE rushes in)

ROSE
Please say you're not angry,
I just couldn't bear it!
Please say you forgive me —
I want you to swear it!

(ALEX's rage dissolves instantly)

ALEX
Of course I'm not angry —
I knew that you'd make it.
There's plenty of time ...

(taking her case)

Here, that's heavy — I'll take it.

ROSE
I feel seventeen again!

ALEX
So do I ...

*(They kiss. A stunned beat. She hands the flowers she
has been carrying to the STATION GUARD, who
has just entered. BOTH hurry off. Dissolve to ...)*

SCENE 5

(Interior of train. Later the same night. ROSE and ALEX, midway on their journey, she lying against him, asleep)

ALEX
Seeing is believing,
And in my arms I see her:
She's here,
Really here,
Really mine now —
She seems at home here . . .

Seeing is believing.
I dreamt that it would be her:
At last
Life is full,
Life is fine now . . .

Whatever happens,
One thing is certain:
Each time I see
A train go by,
I'll think of us,
The night, the sky
Forever . . .

(Time passes. He is now asleep, she awake)

ROSE
He's young,
Very young,
But appealing —
I feel I know him . . .

Seeing is believing,
And I like what I see here.
I like
Where I am,
What I'm feeling . . .

What are we doing?
Can you believe it?
A starving actress and
A star-struck boy —
Oh well, I might
As well enjoy
The moment . . .

(He wakes and they look at one another)

ALEX
Can you believe it?

BOTH
Seeing is believing!
I never thought I'd be here!
Is this
Really me?
Am I dreaming?

No way of knowing
Where this is leading . . .
It's fun forgetting
Who we are . . .
Who cares? When now
The world is far
Behind us . . .

Seeing is believing!
My life is just beginning!
We touched,
And my head
Won't stop spinning,
From winning
Your love!

(They kiss. Dissolve to . . .)

SCENE 6

(GEORGE's villa at Pau. Interior of drawing-room. Night. Pitch black. The glimmer of torchlight. ALEX is trying to prise open the French windows)

ALEX *(outside)*
Wish my arms were longer . . .
Or the gap was wider . . .
One more go and
That should do it . . .
One more try and there —
That does it!

(A crash of breaking wood and glass. They stagger in, throwing torchlight on to the scene)

ROSE
You will rue the day
That you got me in this mess!
I've torn my one good dress!
You're really a charmer!

ALEX
Rose, I know this seems
Like a scene from 'Modern Times' . . .

The house is my uncle's —
All right, I was lying —
He's working in Paris,
He won't come here prying . . .
Oh Rose,
Rose, can't you see?
I would have said anything
To get you here with me . . .

(No reply from her. Nervous, he tries changing tack)

Shall I make some coffee . . . ?

(She suddenly decides to give in, laughing long and loud)

One cup of fresh coffee
Buys two kisses —
Shall we have dinner?

(They touch in the darkness, and kiss)

BOTH
Whatever happens,
We have this moment
Who needs tomorrow,
When we have today?
Tonight we'll mean
The things we say
Forever . . .

Seeing is believing!
My life is just beginning!
We touched,
And my head
Won't stop spinning
From winning
Your love!

(They kiss again in earnest. Dissolve to . . .)

SCENE 7

(An art exhibition in Paris. Among the throng of ARTISTS and GLITTERATI is GIULIETTA TRAPANI, a young Italian sculptress. GEORGE DILLINGHAM, her 58-year-old lover, fights his way to her through the crowd angrily brandishing a telegram)

GEORGE
Damn the boy!
Damn the boy's
Damn-fool schoolboy antics!

GIULIETTA
Calm down now, George . . .

GEORGE *(interrupting, reads:)*
'Nephew Alex break in, stop.
Stealing household supplies, stop.
Living in sin, stop.
Please advise, stop.'
My gardener, Jérôme!

GIULIETTA *(smiles)*
How very nice!
How sweet!

GEORGE
How handy!
My bed!
My brandy!

GIULIETTA
He sounds like you —
I think you ought to introduce us!

GEORGE
Giulietta...
You'd better cancel supper at 'Chez Max' —
This week was fun.
It shouldn't end like this...

GIULIETTA
This interlude was heaven...

GEORGE
How sad to think that it must end
When it had just begun...

GIULIETTA
George, you've got a painter's eye:
Everything is magnified!
I know you're all he's got,
But I don't see why you should go.

GEORGE
No, I must go.
Our little fling has done us good.
I have my paint,
You have your clay:
We both have work...

GIULIETTA
I know, I know.
Don't look so sad, George!
What times we've had, George!

GEORGE
There'll be more...

GIULIETTA
Ah yes.
That's true.
George...
There'll never be another you...
But, as you say, you are his guardian,
And sacrifices must be made.
We must part,
I'm afraid...
So put 'Giulietta' thoughts behind you,
Forget about your broken heart!

(turning away, half to herself)

Back to Venice...
Tend my art...

GEORGE (moving across to her)
A love affair is not a lifetime.
It's calendars and clocks, my friend.
All good things.
Have to end.
A memory of a happy moment —
That's what this week will one day be.
Life goes on,
Love goes free.

(Thrusting the telegram into his pocket, he disappears)

GIULIETTA (alone)
Life goes on...
Love goes free...

(Dissolve to...)

SCENE 8

(Bedroom at Pau. Morning sunlight. ROSE alone at the window, drinking in the view)

ROSE
This is what I ought to feel on stage...
Soaring up like snow-capped mountains...
I feel your beauty and your rage...
I could be those tumbling forests,

I could play those jagged hillsides...
Star of mountain,
Star of valley...

(She rehearses, in mime, the closing lines of The Master Builder. ALEX enters).

ALEX
Would Madam care for breakfast?
Will croissants and fresh coffee do?

(A pause. BOTH gaze at the view)

Wonderful view!
Whenever we see those mountains,
We will think of me and you...

(Another admiring pause)

George insists on magnificent views.

ROSE
I think I should like your uncle...

(Dissolve to...)

SCENE 9

(Exploring sequence covering the whole day. Various locations in GEORGE's house, starting with:)

1/Drawing-room

(Dust-sheets are pulled off furniture. ROSE uncovers a portrait of a young woman in a sumptuous Edwardian ball-gown)

ROSE
Alex, she's beautiful. Who is she?

ALEX
My Aunt Delia. She was an actress too.

ROSE
Delia! Was she famous?

ALEX
Yes. But she died very young. That's why my uncle doesn't come down here very often. Too many memories.

(ROSE uncovers another painting, rather a famous one)

ROSE
Haven't seen that somewhere before?

ALEX
Not the one you're thinking of. That's in the Louvre. George did that one. Some people call it fraud, but he prefers to think of it as a tribute.

2/Hall

(They open a trunk)

ALEX (brandishing a rapier)
En garde!

ROSE (parrying with a tennis racket)
Fifteen love!

BOTH
Promise me today will never end!

3/Kitchen

(Boxes full of food)

ROSE (pulling out various tins)
Caviar! Anchovies! Peaches in brandy! We can have a banquet tonight!

ALEX
When he does get down here, George doesn't believe in having to rough it.

BOTH
I could get to like it here!
Let's not ever think of leaving!

4/Bedroom

(A wardrobe full of fancy-dress costumes)

ALEX
Look at this. Pierrot. Carmen.

(holding up a particularly flimsy one)

For the ballroom? Or the bedroom?

(ROSE produces an old bound volume from a chest)

ROSE
Mérimée, 'L'Occasion'. I know this — it's a wonderful play!

ALEX
Really?

ROSE
Let's do it. You can be the priest, I'll be Doña Maria Colemenares.

ALEX
But I don't know anything about the theatre.

ROSE
I'll teach you. We'll do it. Tonight.

(ALEX takes the book and quotes dramatically:)

ALEX
'What are you doing? Pull yourself together...'

(ROSE has meanwhile pulled out a spectacular ball-gown — the same one featured in the portrait)

ROSE
This one is gorgeous!

ALEX (looking up)
It was her favourite dress...

ROSE
He must have loved her so much.

ALEX
Rose, leave things as they are...

ROSE (holding it up to herself and looking in the mirror)

I can just see her...
I feel I know her...

(Dissolve to...)

SCENE 10

(Terrace at Pau. The figure of GEORGE is seen approaching the house. Voices are heard from inside. ROSE and ALEX appear from the house in costume, rehearsing. GEORGE steps back into the shadows, unseen.)

FATHER EUGENIO (ALEX)
What does this letter contain? Give it to me.

DOÑA MARIA (ROSE)
But promise me not to read it while you are here. Read it this evening — wait till this evening. Promise me. And tomorrow... no, never speak to me about it. If you give it back I shall punish myself for my folly... but for God's sake don't scold me.

FATHER EUGENIO (ALEX)
Hand it over.

DOÑA MARIA (ROSE)
Have pity, I implore you. I have resisted as
long as I could, but you mustn't open it here.
Oh, God, what are you doing? Father
Eugenio, I implore you. For pity's sake, give it
back. Father, you are killing me.

FATHER EUGENIO (ALEX)
What are you doing? Pull yourself together.

*(Suddenly aware of GEORGE's presence, ALEX
spins round. A beat)*

GEORGE
You must forgive this rude intrusion,
But I really felt I had to say 'well done'!

(General embarrassment. No one is sure what to say)

ALEX
Oh, Uncle George,
Come in, come in . . .

ROSE
I've heard a million things about you . . .

GEORGE
And you are . . . ?

ROSE
I am Rose Vibert.

GEORGE
I hate to spoil your fun,
But I'm dying for a gin —
But don't let me disturb you.

ROSE
Oh, it's nice to meet you . . .

GEORGE *(warming to the situation)*
Surely Mérimée's 'L'Occasion'?

ALEX
Lemon?
Ice?

ROSE
The perfect play.

GEORGE
Yet overstated . . .

ROSE
Yes, that's true.

GEORGE
. . . And somehow dated now —
A living fossil!

ROSE
How concise!

GEORGE
And Alex, you show promise.

ROSE
Well, he is my pupil!

GEORGE *(to ROSE)*
Ah, so this is your profession?

ALEX
Rising star!

GEORGE
I'm sure, I'm sure.

ROSE
I'm playing Hilde . . .

ALEX
. . . In two weeks.

GEORGE
'The Master Builder'?

ROSE
Yes.

GEORGE
What a courageous girl you are!

ROSE
I hate to tear myself away,
But I must go and change —
Please promise me you'll stay.

GEORGE
I wouldn't dream of going far!

(She goes. GEORGE turns to ALEX, delighted)

I'd like to be the first
To say 'She's perfect!' —
A face like that
I haven't seen in years!

ALEX
You must forgive us
For breaking in here.
I'll make it up, George,
Have no fear —
But please don't throw
Us out of here,
I beg you . . .
Seeing is believing —
I saw her and I loved her . . .
You must understand what I'm saying —
She's not just someone . . .

GEORGE
A love affair is not a crisis.
Enjoy it like a fine champagne —
Taste, but never let it
Cloud the brain.
A memory of a happy moment —
That's what this time will one day be.
Life goes on,
Love goes free . . .

ALEX
Some girls are like that,
They'll love you and leave you,
But Rose —
There's only one Rose . . .
I'm telling you,
This is not some schoolboy game —
My life will never be the same . . .

GEORGE
I look at you and
I remember
How many times I've
Felt this way —
Ah, the tricks
Love can play . . .

ALEX
I knew it from the moment
That I saw her face . . .
There could
Never be
Any other
Love for me . . .

*(ROSE appears in the doorway. She is wearing
the ball-gown we saw earlier, which lends her a
resplendent, other-worldly quality. For a moment we
half believe we are seeing the portrait come to life.
BOTH turn upstage and see her. The effect on
GEORGE is devastating. Overcome, he stumbles to a
chair)*

GEORGE
Alex, quick!
Some brandy!

(ROSE and ALEX rush over to him)

ROSE
You go . . .

ALEX
I'll go . . .

ROSE
Quickly . . .

ALEX *(hurrying out)*
I'm going . . .

*(He goes. GEORGE recovers himself while ROSE
tends to him)*

GEORGE
Do forgive me . . .
So unlike me . . .
You looked just like her . . .
My wife . . .
Delia . . .
I thought for a moment . . .
The dress was hers,
But you look just as lovely —
It should be worn . . .
I've caused such drama here . . .

ROSE
You mustn't think that . . .

GEORGE
It wasn't meant, my dear . . .
I'd better leave you two alone . . .

(He makes to go. She stops him)

ROSE
You're in no state to travel —
No,
You won't go anywhere.
You're staying in that chair.
Why spend the evening on your own?

*(The scene transforms to reveal ALEX in the kitchen
attending to GEORGE's brandy)*

ALEX
Why, why must he spy on us?
It was perfect till he came!
Why, why must he ruin it?

(Dissolve to . . .)

SCENE 11

*(Terrace at Pau. Later the same evening, ROSE,
GEORGE and ALEX at the tail end of dinner,
ALEX slightly drunk)*

GEORGE
. . . Of course, painting always was my first
love.

ROSE *(to ALEX)*
Why aren't you so gifted.

GEORGE
When I'm dead they'll fetch a fortune.

ALEX
We shall see.

ROSE
I'd buy one now.

ALEX *(to GEORGE)*
You'd better tell her . . .

ROSE
Tell me what?

ALEX
... Before you sell her one,
That they're just copies ...

GEORGE
But by *me!*

ROSE (*changing the subject, to GEORGE*)
I'd love to hear your poems!

GEORGE
I shall write one for you ...

ALEX
Byron isn't here to sue you.

ROSE
Alex, please —
Don't interrupt.

GEORGE
At least I *do* things ...

ROSE
Yes, that's true.

GEORGE
... I see a few things through ...

(*to ROSE*)

We often have disputes like these.

(*then, changing the subject*)

Did Alex ever tell you ...

ALEX
We'll be here till breakfast ...

GEORGE (*ignoring him, continues*)
... Why his final year
At school was rather short?

ROSE
No, not a word.

ALEX (*horrified realization*)
No, George, you couldn't ...

ROSE
Please go on!

ALEX
No, George, you wouldn't dare ...

GEORGE
I think it might amuse her ...

(*He leans over and whispers in ROSE's ear. Her reaction is a long and loud guffaw. ALEX blushes to the roots. A beat. Then GEORGE adds:*)

I've had a splendid time,
A truly splendid time —
But now I really ought to go ...
I have a little tryst
Too tempting to resist,
And I can see that I'm *de trop* ...

(*He rises, then turns back to them*)

I wish you both a charming fortnight,
Enjoy your little one-to-one —
Have your fling,
Have your fun ...

A memory of a happy moment —
That's what these days will one day be ...
Life goes on,
Love goes free ...

(*moving off*)

Life goes on,
Love goes free ...

(*He disappears. ALEX looks after him*)

ALEX
I think I know where he's gone —
He's off to take his Italian lessons!

(*A beat. Suddenly ROSE rounds on ALEX*)

ROSE
How could you have let me wear this dress?
He must think I have no feelings!
You should have said what he was like ...
I must seem a heartless woman!
I must seem a soulless creature!
Anyway, let's not have a scene ...

(*She moves off, heading for bed. Dissolve to ...*)

SCENE 12

(*The terrace. Pitch black. A noise outside has woken ROSE*)

ROSE (*offstage*)
What was that?

ALEX (*offstage*)
What?

ROSE
There.
Listen.
It's her ghost.
I'm frightened.

ALEX (*himself a little scared*)
Don't be silly.
I'll go and have a look.

(*He comes out to investigate*)

ROSE (*from inside*)
Well?

(*We see ALEX on the terrace. He has found a solitary satin ladies' shoe lying there. He cannot remember it being there before. Mystified, he puts the shoe to one side and returns to the house*)

ALEX (*covering his misgivings*)
There's nothing there. I suppose it must have been a rat.

ROSE (*going back in*)
I can't sleep in a house full of rats!

ALEX (*following*)
Well, I don't want you to sleep just yet ...

ROSE
Alex. Not now.

(*Lights fade. Musical interlude carrying us through to morning. ALEX discovered alone, talking in his dream*)

ALEX
Rose, where are you?
Rose, where are you?

(*He wakes with a start to find himself alone. For a few moments he is confused by the apparent overlapping of dream and reality. A moment later ROSE cheerfully bounces in carrying his clothes*)

ROSE
I've been out walking.
And what a day —
So crisp and clear!
And you're not spending it in here!

(*She throws him his clothes*)

Let's breathe some mountain air!

ALEX
I thought you'd left me ...

ROSE (*continuing on her own line of thought*)
What do *you* say?

ALEX
I had a dream you'd left me ...

ROSE
Good idea?

ALEX (*coming to*)
Good idea!

(*Dissolve to ...*)

SCENE 13

(*Various locations in and around the Pyrenees. A brief excursion taking us through the rest of the day. ALEX and ROSE enjoying the idyllic local scenery*)

ROSE
'Pas de tendresse
Et pas de joie,
Loin d'ici,
Loin de toi.

Rien de plus triste
Que mes soupirs,
Lorsque vient le jour
Où il me faut partir.

Chanson d'enfance,
Tu vis toujours dans mon coeur.
Toi, la plus douce!
Toi, la plus tendre!'

(*All is once again perfect. As the day ends, ROSE and ALEX take a final, admiring look at the scene*)

ALEX
What could be sweeter?

BOTH
Nothing is sweeter ...

(*We follow their path homeward, as we dissolve to ...*)

SCENE 14

(*ROSE and ALEX returning to the house. Late afternoon. She notices a telegram lying on the doormat. Slowly picks it up, opens it and reads*)

ROSE
Marcel wants me in Lyon ...
He says that I'm needed today ...

ALEX
Well, it must be important ...

ROSE
I won't go.
I don't want to.
I'll ignore it.

(*She screws up the telegram and throws it aside*)

How can I desert you?
It's all so unfair,
So unfeeling!

ALEX
How can you say that?
Don't be a fool, Rose!
You can't put me before your whole career!
You can't let feelings interfere —
You *must* go!

(She nods and moves tearfully away)

ROSE
I'll pick up my script and my dress.

(She goes. Lights fade, time passes. When next they come up we see ALEX, now alone, pensively wandering about the house. He finds the crumpled telegram and picks it up)

ALEX
'A memory of a happy moment —
That's what this week will one day be . . .'
George . . . you're wrong . . .

(Re-reading, a flash of realization hits him)

Marcel —
How could he have known where she was?
Unless she told him . . .
Or sent this herself . . .
And there was I,
Completely taken in,
When she was going all along . . .

(cries out)

No, she couldn't . . .
Oh God, she wouldn't . . .

(Blackout. Dissolve to . . .)

SCENE 15

(A fairground in Paris, two years later. Early evening. ALEX in military uniform with TWO FELLOW OFFICERS and their TWO GIRLS. ALEX is also accompanied by a GIRL. BARKERS cry their wares from various stalls and PLEASURE-SEEKERS mill about)

RIFLE-RANGE BARKER
Who's feeling lucky?
Twenty out of twenty
And a prize could be yours!

FREAK-SHOW BARKER
See 'Marie the Monkey'
With the poisonous claws!

RIFLE-RANGE BARKER
There's a prize
To be won!

FREAK-SHOW BARKER
Take a risk,
Take a ride!

RIFLE-RANGE BARKER
Right this way,
Have a go!

FREAK-SHOW BARKER
Try your luck
And step inside!

(ALEX is persuaded to try his skill at shooting. As he shoots, the OTHERS sing encouragement.)

CHORUS
If you reach
For the moon,
If you aim
For the sky,
Then the moon
And the sky
Can be yours —
Come on and try!

Everybody loves a hero!
Let's hear it for the man with the gun!
Everybody loves a hero . . .

(ALEX successfully completes the volley. The jackpot is his, and he is handed his prize: a toy donkey)

BARKER
And you, sir,
Are now the proud owner
Of this magnificent donkey!

(General hilarity. The group moves away from the stall)

CHORUS
Everybody loves a hero!
Let's hear it for the man with the gun!
Everybody loves a hero . . .

FRIEND 1 *(to ALEX)*
Two more days . . .

FRIEND 2
Just two more days!

FRIEND 1
. . . And you'll be back
To civvy street again!

FRIEND 3
And decent food.

FRIEND 2
And your life is yours at last!

FRIEND 3
You lucky devil!

GIRLS
Your girlfriend's gonna love that donkey!

ALL
You'll be her hero!

ALEX *(detaching himself from the limpet GIRL)*
Two long years . . .
I had a dream I'd see her name in lights:
Rose Vibert, the shining star!
I've given up trying to find her . . .
Perhaps she's resting . . .

FRIEND 3
So who's the lucky girl tonight, then?

ALEX *(moving off as the scene dissolves)*
I've told you:
It's my uncle.

FRIENDS *(fading into the background)*
Uncle?
Not likely . . .
Give her a kiss from us . . .

(We have by now dissolved to . . .)

SCENE 16

(Living room of GEORGE's flat, later that evening. ELIZABETH, GEORGE's housekeeper, is showing ALEX in)

ELIZABETH
How you've grown!

ALEX
It's been two years.

ELIZABETH
You should have phoned —
Your uncle isn't here.

ALEX
I might have guessed!

ELIZABETH
And such a splendid uniform!

ALEX *(looking around the flat)*
The same old paintings.

ELIZABETH
Madame will be so thrilled to meet you —
I'll go and tell her.

(ALEX picks up a small sculpture, examines it and reads the artist's signature on the base)

ALEX
'Giulietta Trapani' . . .

ELIZABETH *(turning back)*
Life has changed!
Since those two met
He lives life to the full!

ALEX
Well, good for him!

ELIZABETH
She has made him young again!

ALEX
Where is he now, then?

ELIZABETH
He's doing up the country villa —
They plan to live there.
Now, tell me, do you still like omelettes?
Won't be a moment!

(She bustles out. ALEX, alone, wanders about the room, musing)

ALEX
And so he got his wicked way with that
Italian girl —
He hasn't lost his touch . . .

(Placing the toy donkey on a coffee table, he relaxes into a chair. A beat. Very slowly, behind ALEX, ROSE appears. Gently, she speaks)

ROSE
Well, hello . . .

(ALEX turns and sees her)

ALEX
I should have known
Where you were hiding —
You like the good life,
George likes trinkets!
God, what a fool
I was to love you!
What was all my searching for?
It's never hard to find a whore!

ROSE
Well, if it makes you happy, think it . . .

ALEX
You scheming bitch . . .

ROSE
. . . The truth is we're a perfect pair.

ALEX
Because he's rich . . .

ROSE
Shout and scream —
I don't care . . .

ALEX
You could have let me know . . . !

ROSE
Your uncle's shown me new horizons . . .

ALEX
Well, didn't I?

ROSE
And as a lover he is perfect too.

ALEX
Another lie!

ROSE
He takes his time.
Unlike you.

ALEX
I wasn't good enough?

ROSE
Why can't you listen
And come to your senses?
It's George . . .
I really love George . . .
He's made me a
Better, fuller, stronger person,
I have never been as happy!

ALEX
Or, indeed, as wealthy.

ROSE
Look, I don't need your uncle's money!
And I could have a thousand lovers!
Yet I've been faithful and I'm happy —
More faithful than he'll ever be:
It's not as if he's married me . . .

(She turns away, tearful)

ALEX (calming)
I'd better go . . .
I'm sorry . . .
It was a shock . . .

ROSE
Try and understand,
And it won't hurt you so much.

ALEX
At least admit you loved me once . . .

ROSE
Of course I did.
I may even love you now . . .
George gives me so much . . .
But he gets so little from me . . .
Yet with you I made an impression
That will last you a lifetime . . .

ALEX (moving close to her)
So change my life for me again . . .

(Lights fade as, fatally, he kisses her and she leads
him to her bedroom)

SCENE 17

(Living room of GEORGE's Paris flat. Next
morning. The cuddly donkey still sits on the table.
ALEX enters from the bedroom in search of ROSE)

ALEX
Here we go again!
Heaven knows when she'll be back —
That girl has got a knack
Of keeping you guessing!

ELIZABETH (entering flustered)
Madame will soon be here,
But she says you are to leave:
Your uncle is coming,
You'd better get going . . .

ALEX
So why all the panic?
Why shouldn't I be here?

ELIZABETH
She's scared that his heart
Couldn't stand all this drama . . .

ALEX
Well, it's hardly a shock
If my uncle sees me here . . .

(Elizabeth hurries out)

That girl is unbelievable!
Was last night the sort of thing
She could just forget?
It would be hard to find
A more capricious mind . . .

(ROSE bursts in and is instantly infuriated to see
him still there)

ROSE
What are you doing here?

ALEX
All right, where have you been?

ROSE
Will you please disappear?

ALEX
What the hell do you mean?

ROSE (turns away)
Leave me, leave me!
I don't want George exposed
To some unpleasant scene.

(She walks over to the gramophone and puts on a
record, casually, halfway through. It is 'Parlez-vous
français?' To ALEX this is red rag to a bull)

ALEX (getting out his gun)
If I can't have you, no one will.
Killing you would be a pleasure.

ROSE
So all you're fit for is to kill?
Go on and pull the trigger,
See if I care!
Come on, soldier!
Be a hero!

ALEX
You never loved me?
You never meant it?
And now you hate me . . .

ROSE
Does it matter?
Who remembers?
Go away, you little
Schoolboy . . .

(Enraged, she suddenly seizes a heavy candlestick and
hurls it at him, causing his gun to go off. She is shot
in the arm and a painting hanging behind him falls to
the floor. The gramophone needle jumps and the record
starts to repeat itself.

Hearing the shot, ELIZABETH rushes in
brandishing a hammer with which she hits ALEX on
the elbow, knocking the gun out of his hand. She goes
to the aid of ROSE who has passed out.

No sooner has this happened than GEORGE enters
the flat. He takes the needle off the stuck record. He
glances at the spectacle of this 'crime passionel' and
then he sees the displaced painting. He hurries across
to inspect it)

GEORGE
My only genuine Matisse!
Thank God . . .
No damage done . . .

Would someone kindly tell me
What on earth has happened?

ELIZABETH
He lost his head,
The gun went off,
She's bleeding badly,
Use your scarf —
Here, let me help . . .

(They kneel down beside ROSE and tend to her
wound. ALEX approaches tentatively)

GEORGE
You'd better phone the doctor.

(She turns away from ALEX, who turns to
GEORGE)

ALEX
I should never have come back here . . .

GEORGE
Oh, don't talk such nonsense!

ALEX
I'll bow out now —
It's the decent thing to do.

GEORGE
Don't be absurd.

ALEX
I'm a disaster . . .

GEORGE
Oh, come, come!

ALEX
. . . It wouldn't last a week —
She'd be far better off with you.

GEORGE
You two have your lives before you.

ALEX
It would end in murder . . .

GEORGE
I'm too old for her —
It's high time I withdrew.

ALEX
Your place is here.

GEORGE
The jowls are dropping . . .

ALEX
It's the light.

GEORGE
. . . The paunch needs propping up —
She'd be far better off with you.

BOTH
Your words are generous and selfless,
But alas untrue —
She'd be far better off with you.

ALEX
You are steeped in wit and wisdom.

GEORGE
Well, I've learnt the odd thing . . .

ALEX
You could teach George Bernard Shaw
A thing or two!

GEORGE
I had a go . . .

(ROSE leaves the room, helped by ELIZABETH)

ALEX
You've dined with Garbo . . .

GEORGE
Only twice.

ALEX
... Translated 'La Bohème' —
She'd be far better off with you.

GEORGE
You're athletic.

ALEX
You're distinguished.

GEORGE
You don't cheat at croquet.

ALEX
You're more seasoned.

GEORGE
You can skate.

ALEX
You're in 'Who's Who'.

GEORGE
Just half an inch.

ALEX
We're talking drivel.

GEORGE
So we are.

BOTH
Can't we be civilized?
She'd be far better off with you.
Your words are generous and selfless,
But alas untrue.
It's only Rose that matters!
Just take a look: there's no comparison
Between us two —
She'd be far better off with you!

GEORGE
You're too young
And too confused
To understand what's best,
And what's best is obvious:
The two of you belong together —
There'll be less damage!

ALEX
Perhaps you're right —
I'll do my best
To turn our lives around
And brush away this memory.

GEORGE
I'll phone you when I get to Venice.

ALEX
Giulietta?

(GEORGE makes no reply, but instead casts a wistful final gaze about the room)

GEORGE
Now you be good to her ...
I have to say these were
The sweetest days I've ever known ...

ALEX
Well, have a pleasant journey ...

GEORGE
One thing before I go,
Just one thing you should know:
Rose doesn't like to be alone ...

(He leaves, ELIZABETH re-enters the living room. She rounds furiously on ALEX)

ELIZABETH
You're a delinquent.
A silly schoolboy with a gun.
Take a look at what you've done.
I hope you're satisfied.

ROSE (re-entering)
Goodbye, Alex.
Goodbye forever.
We've packed your tunic,
Here's your gun as well.
So, blow your brains out,
Go to hell,
Just leave me.

ALEX (stunned)
You don't know what you're saying ...

ROSE
I've phoned Marcel.
To see you off.

(MARCEL enters. With decisiveness masking his fear, he hurries ALEX along)

MARCEL
Come along,
Get marching.
Double-quick,
Look lively.

ALEX
Let me see ...
My suitcase ...

(He goes, MARCEL following)

ROSE (momentarily alone)
Will he ever forgive me?
But what can I do?
I'm in love with them both ...
But I only have one life,
Not two ...

(MARCEL re-enters)

MARCEL
Your life is one enormous drama!
My God, you'll be the death of me!

(examining her wound)

What a mess ...
Let me see ...

A memory that is best forgotten —
That's what this ugly scene should be.
Life goes on,
So must we ...

(ROSE meanwhile has picked up from the desk a letter. She reads aloud the name of the sender)

ROSE
'Trapani ...'

Marcel, we're taking a trip.
I'm told that Venice is fun.
We have to meet an Italian lady ...

(Dissolve. During the scene change we see GEORGE arriving in Venice, being greeted by an overjoyed GIULIETTA and re-establishing his relationship with her)

SCENE 18

(GIULIETTA's studio in Venice. Some days later. GEORGE sitting for a sculpture of him on which GIULIETTA is working, at the same time giving her his vision of events in Paris)

GEORGE
... And then with a swift karate-chop
I removed his gun —
You should have been there!
Poor chap didn't know what hit him ...

GIULIETTA (interrupting)
Still, George!
If you can't keep your tongue still,
You will have the face of Edith Sitwell!

GEORGE
Ah well, they're happy ...
It's for the best anyway ...
Let's face it,
He's the man for her,
And I'm the man for you, dear ...

GIULIETTA
Don't talk such nonsense —
You'll never stop loving her.
You don't fool me:
You're quite besotted with her ...

(attention back on her work, pleased with his pose)

Stop. Wait. Good. Please ...
Still, George ...

GEORGE
With my scarf I made a tourniquet —
Shantung silk, but worth the sacrifice —
It stemmed the flow, the arm was saved,
and ...

GIULIETTA
Still, George,
Rose would seem the kind of lady
Who would live through any blood-bath ...

GEORGE
Darling, it's over —
So don't be so cynical.
I don't suppose that you've become a nun
Since last I saw you ...

GIULIETTA
Wouldn't you love that!
Perpetual chastity!

GEORGE
So tell me,
Have you found some young Adonis?

GIULIETTA (back to work again)
Stop. Wait. Good. Please ...
No, George.

BOTH
Time and light are fading —
Shouldn't we make the most of
Every precious moment?
Life is sweet and slow and still and ...

(They are interrupted by a babble of voices outside the door, rising in volume. We can just make out the following voices)

VOICES
I'm not leaving here till I get what I came for
... it's a scandal ... out of my way ... heaven
help him if he won't pay ... who are you
pushing ... I got here first ... all I want is
what's fair ... he had better be there ...

GEORGE (over the voices)
For heaven's sake!
Who's making all that mayhem?

(He rises to be greeted by the entrance of MARCEL, closely followed by an angry crowd of people, numbering a HOTELIER, a DOCTOR, a

HOTEL CASHIER, a PHARMACIST and a
GONDOLIER. Together they burst into the
room, all apparently demanding money from
the bewildered GEORGE)

MARCEL *(to GEORGE)*
Thank God you're here!
We've got trouble with Rose —
Running up bills
Wherever she goes!
(to the OTHERS)
This is the man I was
Looking for,
This is your man!

DOCTOR *(to MARCEL)*
Can you be certain that
This is the man?
Is this the right man?

CASHIER *(to HOTELIER)*
This is the man
Who will pay for
The eight-one phone-calls!

(to GEORGE)

I beg of you, pay!
My poor mother is dying!
If I lose my job, then . . .

PHARMACIST *(to DOCTOR)*
This is the man
Who will pay for
The codeine and dressings!

(to GEORGE)

HOTELIER *(to
MARCEL)*
Are you certain that
This is the man?

Is he the one
Footing the bill?
Is this the man?

HOTELIER *(to
GEORGE)*
She loses her job if
These bills don't get
settled!

We'll call the police if . . .

CASHIER
The Doge's Suite!

HOTELIER
Beluga caviar!

GONDOLIER
You are the man,
I understand,
Who can clear my expenses.
Here they are:
Thirty thousand lire!

*(All of them present GEORGE with their bills. He
and GIULIETTA attempt between them to assemble
the cash needed to clear the various accounts)*

CASHIER
Forty thousand!

HOTELIER
Fifty thousand!

DOCTOR & PHARMACIST
Twenty thousand lire!

GONDOLIER
Thirty thousand lire!

CASHIER
Forty thousand!

HOTELIER
Fifty thousand!

*(GEORGE settles the last bill. MARCEL turns to
him apologetically)*

DOCTOR *(to
GEORGE)*
I've called the
police, there
Are eight in the
lobby!

DOCTOR &
PHARMICIST
Twenty thousand
lire!

GEORGE *(counting)*
Nineteen . . .

GIULIETTA
(counting)
Twenty-three . . .

GEORGE &
GIULIETTA
Forty-eight . . .
Forty-nine . . .

MARCEL
George, I'm sorry . . . She's been very ill.

(The crowd now parts to admit ROSE, the cause of all the confusion, supported by a NUN. She is ailing and delirious from the gun-shot wound)

ROSE
George . . . George . . .
My life is draining . . .
Away . . .

(She collapses into an armchair and passes out. The crowd, ushered away by GEORGE, withdraws, MARCEL following)

MARCEL *(backing out, to GEORGE)*
We'd best be on our way —
We'll leave you three alone . . .

(He goes)

GIULIETTA
So this is Rose Vibert.
The famous Rose Vibert.

GEORGE
I have to talk to her.
Sit down and talk to her.
This can't go on another day.

(He looks at ROSE who begins to recover)

Rose, what can I do with you?
Wreaking havoc left and right —
It's absurd!
She must change her ways,
She must pass this passing phase —
Problem child . . .
Running wild . . .

Rose, I ought to strangle you!
But there's a style about that girl
That stops me in my tracks.
Heaven knows why she
Wants to waste her life with me . . .

And yet if she went off,
If she set herself free,
As I've told her she should . . .
Where on earth would I be?

GIULIETTA
You'd be lost, my friend,
And so would she . . .

(With a sad smile, she looks away. Dissolve to . . .)

SCENE 19

(The same. About two weeks later. Late afternoon. ROSE is propped up on a couch. GIULIETTA is sketching her)

ROSE
. . . And he said to me
He really ought to buy that vineyard . . .

GIULIETTA
Please, Rose.
Don't you think you ought
To take a little rest
From George's foibles?

ROSE
Well, you'll have to learn to live with it.
That and all his other pet obsessions:
God and Trollope,
Other women . . .

GIULIETTA
Please, Rose!

(then, more serious)

George is a remarkable man.
He was there when I thought I had no one.
He saw me through my darkest moments.
He made me talk about my husband.

(thinking back)

We had been married five days . . .
He drove like the wind . . .
Not any more . . .

(turning back to ROSE)

. . . But George was always there,
No matter when or where.
He stopped me feeling so alone . . .

(A pause)

ROSE
When did you meet him?

GIULIETTA
One evening in Harry's bar —
He wore a silver tie pin
And a smile that was even brighter . . .

(She smiles, recollecting. ROSE returns the smile)

ROSE
I know that tie pin —
It catches on *everything*!

GIULIETTA
And as for all those paint rags . . .

ROSE
Heaven help us!

BOTH
We deserve a medal!

(BOTH laugh. A bond seems to be developing between them. ROSE glances about the room, which is strewn with the debris of GEORGE's occupation)

ROSE
Nice to see that George has settled in:
Fifteen novels on the go, as always!
Used to drive me to distraction . . .

GIULIETTA
Please, Rose!

(then, with a smile)

Last year he forgot my birthday,
So I rearranged his bookmarks . . .

(They laugh again. GEORGE wanders in)

ROSE
George dear, we're talking —
We don't need you hovering.

GIULIETTA
My darling, you're completely right —

(to GEORGE)

We're doing fine without you.

GEORGE *(smiles)*
I get the picture.
Condemn me to solitude!

ROSE
You'll find some things to keep you occupied.

GIULIETTA
We'll call you if we need you!

(GEORGE leaves)

ROSE & GIULIETTA
Time and light are fading —
Shouldn't we make the most
Of every precious moment?
Life is sweet and slow and still
And perfect!
All the more, now our man George
Has brought the two of us together!
. . . (Dissolve to . . .)

SCENE 20

(Beside a canal in Venice. Daytime. GEORGE reads a letter and is clearly disturbed by the contents. ROSE, her arm still in a sling, joins him)

ROSE
I never imagined she'd be like that —
Your lady friend comes as a sweet
surprise . . .
A wonderfully sweet surprise . . .

GEORGE
Take a deep breath and prepare yourself . . .
I've been such a trusting fool . . .
Those wretched investments I made
Have gone down the drain . . .
After today, there'll be no more
champagne . . .
The ways of the world are cruel . . .

ROSE
If I ask a question . . .
Will you promise . . . ?
You must promise . . .
That the answer to my question is 'yes' . . .

GEORGE
Yes, I'll say yes . . .

ROSE
Take a deep breath and prepare yourself . . .
My mind is in such a mess . . .
But really, George,
All that I wanted to ask was this:
Would you be willing to marry me?

GEORGE
I've already told you.
Yes.

(A beat. They embrace. Dissolve to . . .)

SCENE 21

(A registry office in Venice. Afternoon. The wedding of GEORGE and ROSE. GEORGE, ROSE, MARCEL, a REGISTRAR and various GUESTS. We cut in at the very end of the ceremony)

REGISTRAR
'. . . I now pronounce you man and wife.'

(General merriment. MARCEL steps forward and kisses both of them)

MARCEL
My dears, congratulations!

GUEST 1
Here's to the happy couple!

MARCEL
Here's to happy days!
And even better nights!

GUEST 2
You lucky man!

GEORGE *(turning to ROSE with a grin)*
Well, now we've done it!

ROSE
And oh, what fun it was . . .

GIULIETTA *(advancing on ROSE)*
And now I claim my best man's rights!

(And with that she kisses ROSE full and passionately on the lips. All look on. Reactions vary, but GEORGE is clearly highly delighted. He claps his hands and exclaims:)

GEORGE
Bravo, bravo!

(Dissolve to . . .)

SCENE 22

(A military encampment in the Malayan jungle. Some months later. Evening. ALEX composing a letter)

ALEX *(deadpan)*
'News takes time to reach us here.
So you're married.
How times flies.
And George will be a father soon.
That was more of a surprise.
Perhaps one day we'll meet again,
If I ever leave the army . . .'

(He breaks off)

Live or perish
In its flame,
Love will never,
Never let you
Be the same . . .

(The frozen image of GEORGE, ROSE and GIULIETTA, in triptych, disappears from view, leaving ALEX alone)

Love will never,
Never let you
Be the same!

(He goes)

END OF ACT ONE

Act Two

Orchestral Introduction to Act Two

SCENE 1

(A theatre in Paris. Some 12 years later. View from backstage. A performance of Turgenev's A Month in the Country, *a triumphant last night. ROSE, now 39, is alone on stage, starring as NATALIA PETROVNA)*

NATALIA *(ROSE)* Natalia Petrovna ...
Unhappy woman, for the first time in your life
... you are in love.

(Cut to the end of the play. Tumultuous applause ringing in her ears, ROSE comes off stage and makes her way through a throng of backstage visitors, to her dressing-room. MARCEL pushes to the fore and embraces her)

MARCEL
If Turgenev were here
He'd order champagne!
A triumph, my dear!

ROSE
What a night to end with ...

MARCEL
Rose, you were incredible!

ROSE
They seemed to like it ...

MARCEL
I have never heard a crowd
Make a noise like that!

A PASSING VISITOR *(clapping MARCEL on the shoulder)*
It's your best production!

MARCEL *(to ROSE, continuing)*
Are we in the mood
For debauchery and food?

ROSE
Marcel, you are a dear
But a most forgetful man!
I've told you that I plan
To drive to the country.

(We have by this time reached the dressing-room. VISITORS and ADMIRERS cluster in the room offering congratulations)

VISITORS *(severally)*
Well done, darling ...
Well done you ...

ROSE *(to MARCEL, continuing)*
Have a lovely night!
Come and see me when you can.

(She turns to HUGO LE MEUNIER, her young current admirer, who is at her heels)

Now, come along, Hugo

HUGO
I'm ready, don't worry.
I've done all the packing,
There's no need to hurry.

GUEST 1
Tonight was a wonder!

GUEST 2
A soaring sensation!

ROSE
The best thing is having
My friends' admiration

(Silence falls as MARCEL begins his encomium)

MARCEL
The perfect leading lady:
Unique and true and towering!
Magnetic, overpowering!
The star the crowds adore!

If they could only know you:
Your humour and humility ...
Your strength and your fragility ...
They'd love you even more ...

Tonight was a wonder!
All the dreams we worked for
Have come true!
My shining leading lady!
Bravo, bravo, bravo!
I owe so much to you.

(MARCEL now beckons forward a figure lurking in the background. It is the 30-year-old ALEX)

MARCEL
Now, to top it
All, you'll never guess
Who's turned up —
You'll never recognize him!
Twelve years on and still as handsome ...

ROSE *(oblivious)*
Later —
Don't I ever get a minute to myself?
I'll see him later.

(She turns, sees ALEX)

Alex!

(to MARCEL)

It's Alex!

(to ALEX)

How long have you been standing there?

(to MARCEL)

You *are* a fool!
You should have told me!

(to ALEX)

Come on, let me see you!

ALEX
You were amazing!
Now *that's* more like an audience!
This time I must have been the only one
Who didn't throw you roses!

ROSE
Now Hugo, be a dear
And get our guest an Armagnac.

It's on the bottom shelf —
Why not have one yourself?

(She turns to ALEX, smiles, lost for words)

ROSE
Where to start?

ALEX
It's been so long ...

ROSE
Come, have a seat and tell me all your news!

ALEX
Let me see ...

ROSE
George will love to hear it all!

ALEX
How *is* my uncle?

ROSE
He's at the house in Pau with Jenny.
They really love it.
I can't wait
To leave all this and be with them again!
No more stuffy dressing-rooms!

(to HUGO)

Tell Jean-Michel to bring my car round.

(back to ALEX)

We leave this evening.

(then, on impulse)

It's such a long and lonely journey —
Why not come with me ...?

ALEX *(after a pause)*
Are you sure you want me to accept?

(No reply)

Very well, then.
I accept.

(Still no reply. ALEX smiles)

... Here. Have some Armagnac.

(She drinks and returns the glass. He too takes a sip.)

ROSE
Hugo, I'm afraid that your trip is cancelled.

ALEX *(to ROSE)*
Let me just make a very quick phone-call.

HUGO
I know how it is with old friends ...

ROSE *(to HUGO)*
Well, join us by train in a week.

(Attention focuses on ALEX telephoning)

ALEX *(into the phone)*
Janet?
Janet, it's me here.
Look, I don't think I can make it.
It's not that I don't love you, but ...

(At which point we realize that she has hung up. ROSE catches his eye and smiles.)

ALEX
So who exactly *is* this Hugo?

ROSE
So who exactly is this Janet?

(Both laugh. Dissolve to . . .)

SCENE 2

(Outside the stage door at the theatre. The wall is covered with posters of ROSE. ROSE and ALEX appear)

ROSE *(looking up at the posters)*
Have I changed?

ALEX
No, not at all.

ROSE
You're too polite.
This face has had its day.

ALEX
Don't be so silly!

ROSE
Is it 'General Alex' yet?

ALEX
I hardly think so.

ROSE
Two weeks without a script or camera!
I can't believe it!
And then another madcap movie . . .

(a throwaway)

With Monsieur Cocteau . . .
George is sweet.
He says I'm like his favourite Jurançon:
Very strong and beautiful —
But hardly very sweet or subtle,
and not too heady . . .

ALEX
His head must be extremely strong, then —
I'm drunk already!
What a life!

ROSE
You're telling me!

ALEX
What does Jenny make of all this fame?

ROSE
Ask her yourself.

ALEX
Do you think I *ought* to come?

ROSE
My darling, you've become so bourgeois —
We'll have to change that!

(ALEX moves towards her and attempts to kiss her)

ROSE *(turning away)*
The same old Alex . . .
I should be flattered . . .
You're never one to let a chance slip by . . .

ALEX
I'll never understand you till the day I die . . .

BOTH
I'm sorry . . .

(They look at each other and smile. Dissolve to . . .)

SCENE 3

(The terrace at Pau. We discover GEORGE, now in his seventies, urging his 12-year-old daughter, JENNY, to go to bed)

JENNY
I think by now I'm old enough
To put myself to bed.
Why don't you go and forge
Another masterpiece instead?

GEORGE
Oh, Jenny, you're a monster!
I should have had a son!
It seems, alas, a father's lot . . .

BOTH *(she chiming in, as it is a line she has heard often before)*
. . . Is not a happy one!

JENNY
You know I need my donkey.

GEORGE
Why can't you just count sheep?

(hands her the animal)

All right, you have your donkey —
Now will you go to sleep?

JENNY
I'm really thrilled for Mummy!
Weren't they wonderful reviews?
She'll be the toast of Paris!
Mummy's always in the news!

GEORGE
You're right, it is amazing
How the work keeps flooding in,
With appearances in London
And movies in Berlin.

JENNY
Now off you go to bed —
I'll wake you when I hear the car!

GEORGE
Look, Jenny, go to bed —
God, what a chatterbox you are!

(She relents and goes off to bed. GEORGE sits on the terrace, musing)

Jenny
You're a miracle!
Is there nothing you conceal?
Jenny,
You astonish me!
Never hiding
What you feel . . .

Other pleasures . . .
And I've known many . . .
Afternoons
In warm Venetian squares,
Brief encounters,
Long siestas . . .
Pleasures old and new
Can't compare with you.

You amaze me!
Where did you come from?
You do things
Champagne could never do.
Crystal winters,
Crimson summers . . .
Other pleasures . . .
I would trade them all
For you.

Pleasures old and new
Can't compare with you . . .

Wild mimosa . . .
The scent of evening . . .
Shuttered rooms
With sunlight breaking through . . .
Crazy soirées . . .
Lazy Sundays . . .
Other pleasures . . .
I would trade them all
For you.

Sailing off
In the night
On a silver lake . . .
Taking more
From this life
Than I ought to take . . .
Other pleasures . . .
I would trade them all
For you.

(As he is about to doze off, Jenny rushes in)

JENNY
Quickly!
She's here now!
Don't be an old lazybones!

GEORGE *(coming to and looking at his watch)*
Good Lord!
The time!
For once she's managed
To arrive ahead of schedule!

(ROSE enters with luggage. JENNY rushes over to her. Embraces and hellos)

ROSE *(to JENNY, producing a gift-wrapped present)*
And wait till you see
What I've got for you,
Darling.

(hugs her, then turns to GEORGE)

And wait till *you* see
What I've got for you . . .

(And in comes ALEX. Stunned, he surveys the old, familiar scene and finally sees GEORGE)

ALEX
I don't believe this . . .

ROSE *(echoing him)*
I don't believe this . . .

GEORGE *(struggles with his emotions)*
Good God, I wondered what had happened to you!
Rose, you really should have let me know!

(to ALEX)

Dear boy, you must meet Jenny!

ALEX
Hello, cousin.
Nice to meet you.

JENNY
So you're the soldier?

ROSE
This is Alex.
You remember.

JENNY
Yes, of course.

ROSE *(to GEORGE)*
He saw my last performance.

ALEX
She really was phenomenal

JENNY
'A truly blazing star'!

GEORGE, JENNY & ALEX
Rose, you're a wonder!

GEORGE
All the dreams we've worked for
Have come true!

(They go into the house. Dissolve to ...)

SCENE 4

(An open-air café in Venice. GIULIETTA alone, letter-writing)

GIULIETTA
'Big surprise:
I can't be with you this weekend.
But don't be cross —
You should thank me.
You wouldn't find me much fun.
It seems my life is one enormous drama!
Men are such a dreadful nuisance ...
I'll call you when I'm me again.
C'est la vie,
C'est l'amour ...'

(She stops writing and reflects)

There is more to love,
So much more,
Than simply making love —
That's easy.

Gazing into eyes,
Pretty eyes,
Which could be any eyes —
That's crazy.

Hands are just hands,
A face is just a face ...
They come and go —
They're easy to replace ...

There is more to love,
So much more,
That moon-struck escapades —
That's nothing

There is peace of mind,
So much peace,
In quiet company —
That's something.

Everyone but him
Seems wrong for me ...
Every time I feel
There has to be
More ...

If I could hear
The music I heard then,
I'd never let
It fade away again ...

Now each time
Love reaches out to me,
I can only feel
There has to be
So much more
To love ...

There is more to love,
So much more ...

SCENE 5

(Terrace at Pau. A few days later. ROSE, GEORGE, JENNY and ALEX at the end of lunch)

GEORGE *(to ALEX)*
I trust you're staying for the vintage?

JENNY *(to GEORGE)*
Oh, he mustn't miss it!

ROSE
Alex, promise me you won't run off just yet!

JENNY
There's lots of room!

ALEX *(shrugs and smiles)*
I'm in no hurry —
If it won't worry you ...
This could be something you'll regret!

(ROSE has been reading a letter. She suddenly bursts out with:)

ROSE
Oh, no!
That's really disappointing!

GEORGE
What on earth's the matter?

ROSE
Giulietta won't be with us this weekend.

GEORGE
What's happened now?

ROSE
Same situation.

GEORGE
That girl's relationships
Are too involved to comprehend!

ALEX
Looks like I'll never meet your friend.

GEORGE *(rising)*
One day you will, old chap.

(to ROSE)

It's time I took my nap.

(looks at his watch)

Good Lord, the time has really flown!

(He leaves. ROSE also rises)

ROSE
I'd better run along.
You'll have to manage on your own!

(She goes. ALEX and JENNY are left alone. He walks into the sunlight, JENNY watching him)

ALEX *(to himself)*
Part of me was always in these hills ...
This is where my eyes were opened ...
When life was young and we had time ...
I wonder why she brought me back here ...
Why invite me?
Why entice me?
Why rekindle old emotions ...?

(JENNY, idly combing her hair, sings quietly to herself:)

JENNY
I am a mermaid
With golden hair ...

(ALEX, coming out of his day-dream, turns and smiles)

ALEX
I've never seen one like you!

JENNY
Not all us mermaids
Have silver tails —
I have no tail at all.

ALEX
Well, I've never
Seen any mermaids
With knobbly knees!
I'd say this tale
Was a touch too tall,
Maybe a touch too tall ...

JENNY
Sailors would smash on
My jagged rock,
Lured by my siren's song ...

ALEX
It isn't the
Song of the siren
That tortures men —
That's where your theory
Goes sadly wrong,
That's where it all goes wrong ...

JENNY
I thought you'd know better.
You know nothing
About mermaids

ALEX *(wry)*
You know nothing
About sailors...

JENNY
I do!
Much more than you!
If you were a sailor
And heard my song.
Would you be lured by me?

ALEX
I wouldn't be
Foolish enough to
Go near your rock —
I'd steer my galleon out to sea...

BOTH
... Lonely and lost at sea...

(GEORGE comes back, sees them, then looks around)

GEORGE *(muttering to himself)*
Has somebody stolen my copy of 'Brave New World'?
Why can't that woman leave things alone?
My patience is wearing thin...

(He gives up the search, irritated)

Sorry for barging in...

(He leaves. JENNY and ALEX exchange smiles. Dissolve to...)

SCENE 6

(Estate, farms, vineyards, countryside around Pau. Various locations, cinematically unfolding.

A sequence of idyllic summer days, focusing on JENNY and ALEX. They are evidently spending a lot of time together, becoming friends. He more and more embraces the pastoral life, becoming increasingly rustic in dress.

ALEX becomes a more and more frequent visitor to the house at Pau.

The scene culminates at the end of a period of almost three years, when we see ALEX meeting the now 14-year-old JENNY.

Dissolve to...)

SCENE 7

(Outside the house. Late afternoon. ALEX and JENNY relaxing after a long day of walking and talking. Bored with her reading, she steals up on him mischievously and pins him down in a wrestling hold)

JENNY
Say the word!
Say it now!
Nice and loud!

ALEX *(defeated)*
What the hell, then —
Uncle!

(She frees him)

Jenny you're a monster!
You ought to be locked up!

JENNY *(going into the house)*
Before I am,
I think I'll dress for dinner —
You mix the drinks...

(ALEX notices ROSE who has witnessed the latter part of their high jinks)

ALEX *(looking after JENNY)*
She needs a Paris education.
I've told you time and time again.

ROSE
And wouldn't that be cosy?
You could then have your very own
Parisienne!
Alex, how can you even think
Of moving her away from this place?
I mean, Alex, you of all people have found
That leaving here is hard to face.

ALEX
Yes, I love it here and always will...
But Rose, it's not the views
Or the vines that keep me here...
I stay year after year
For something far deeper...
Being in the house
Makes the past seem very near...

BOTH
... When the world was a playground
All train-rides and laughter,
And love in the morning ...

ROSE
... And Armagnac after...

ALEX
Since leaving the army
And being around you,
I know I'm reliving
The night that I found you...

ROSE
But George...
I couldn't hurt George...
Oh Alex, you know by now
How much I love him...

ALEX
So what is it
You feel for Hugo?

ROSE
Please understand I'm not in love with him.
He's a friend. He makes me laugh...
That's all it is.
Alex, can't you see
That you mean much more to me?

Alex, that's why I won't
Play the lover with you.
What I did to you once
Wasn't easy to do —
But I only have one life,
Not two...

(Dissolve to...)

SCENE 8

(Outside on the terrace at Pau. Early summer evening. GEORGE alone, enjoying the evening air)

GEORGE *(murmurs to himself)*
What could be sweeter?
Nothing is sweeter...

(ALEX appears)

When the time comes,
The hour of darkness,
When the light
Is fading from the sky...
When that time comes,
I'll be ready.
Death can hold no fear:
I've done my living *here*.

Earthly pleasures...
And I've known many...
All my life
I've always lived for now.
Who needs heaven?
This is heaven...
When that time comes,
It isn't hard if you
Know how...

(ALEX and GEORGE clasp hands, then ROSE and HUGO wander in. GEORGE smiles at them)

Glass of champagne and endless sunset!
These are the times that life was made for!

ALEX *(gazing at the view)*
Hard to believe that I'd forgotten
Just how perfect life can be —
This magic place has rescued me!

HUGO
The only one not here is Jenny —
I might have known that she'd be late!

GEORGE
She'll be here —
We can wait...

ALEX
She said she had to 'dress for dinner' —
She's talked about it half the week!
What a girl...

HUGO
Quite unique!

GEORGE
Far too advanced for rural classrooms —
She needs the education Paris offers.

ALEX
George, I am in complete agreement —
Paris is the place to learn.

(to ROSE)

I can't say I share *your* concern.

ROSE
The pair of you talk so much nonsense —

(to GEORGE)

She's better here and so are you.
What a pair!
Not a clue!

(JENNY now makes her 'grand entrance', radiant in the same ball-gown which ROSE had worn fifteen years ago. She looks approvingly at the champagne)

JENNY *(so sophisticated)*
Veuve Cliquot...
How divine...

(ROSE and ALEX gesture at her to go back before GEORGE turns and sees her. The shock of seeing the past revisited may this time prove too much for him. But it is too late, he turns. To their astonishment he shows no sign of remembering anything and exhibits nothing but delight at this vision)

GEORGE
I want to be
The first man you remember,
I want to be
The last man you forget.
I want to be
The one you always turn to,
I want to be
The one you won't regret.
May I be first
To say you look delightful?
May I be first
To dance you round the floor?
The very first
To see your face by moonlight?
The very first
To walk you to your door?

JENNY *(playing to GEORGE)*
Well, young man, I'd be delighted!
There is nothing I would rather do!
What could be a sweeter memory
Than sharing my first dance with you?

GEORGE
I want to be
The first man you remember . . .

JENNY
The very first
To sweep me off my feet.

GEORGE
I want to be
The one you always turn to . . .

JENNY
The first to make
My young heart miss a beat.

(He gently takes her in a dance hold and they tentatively try a few steps around the terrace)

GEORGE
Seems the stars are far below us . . .

JENNY
The moon has never felt so close before . . .

(looking up at GEORGE)
Our first dance will be forever . . .

GEORGE
And may it lead to many more!
I want to be
The first man you remember . . .

JENNY
The very first
To sweep me off my feet.

GEORGE
I want to be
The one you always turn to . . .

JENNY
The first to make
My young heart miss a beat.

(Once again they 'take to the floor', this time in a fuller, more formal dance.
The atmosphere is dreamlike and beguiling, and ROSE and HUGO are drawn into the dance. ALEX declines JENNY's attempts to draw him into the dance as well. At the end of the sequence GEORGE leads JENNY back to his seat, and the dance dissolves)

GEORGE
I want to be
The one you always turn to,
I want to be
The one you won't regret . . .

GEORGE & JENNY
The very first . . .
The very first . . .

(Dissolve to . . .)

SCENE 9

(The same. Two hours later, after dinner. JENNY and ALEX alone. She is puzzled by the earlier alarm which greeted her arrival)

JENNY
Now what on earth
Was all that shaking heads for?
Grown-ups are strange —
They're not grown up at all!

ALEX
That dress belonged to George's first wife . . .
Someone should have said before tonight . . .
Years ago your mother wore it —
Your father fainted at the sight . . .

JENNY
Will you be last
To dance with me this evening!
One final dance
Before you run away?

ALEX
It's very late —
But since it's you who's asking,
One final dance
Would crown the perfect day!

(They dance. JENNY begins to hold ALEX in an intimate adult way, when ROSE interrupts them)

ROSE
You shameless pair,
So this is what you're up to.

ALEX
Our game is up —
We might as well come clean!

(He shrugs to JENNY, kisses both goodnight and leaves. JENNY looks after him intently. Then turns to ROSE)

JENNY
He is the first
To make me feel a woman . . .
The very first
To make me fall in love . . .

(ROSE remains silent, studying her face)

The very first . . .
The very first . . .

(JENNY turns away from her mother. Their pose remains. Dissolve to . . .)

SCENE 10

(The vineyard at Pau. Summer evening. HUGO, ALEX and several workmen relaxing with wine after a day of hard manual labour: they have been building a stone wall in the vineyard. ROSE and GEORGE have come down to join them)

LABOURERS 1
Now that's what I call a wall!

LABOURERS 2
It's a masterpiece!

ALEX
It's Picasso!

JENNY
Except it's straight . . .

GEORGE
Hugo, we should call you Samson!

JENNY
He has many talents!

GEORGE *(to ALEX)*
How you didn't break your back I'll never know!

ALEX
No, nor will I!

HUGO
Thank God for Sundays!

ALEX *(appraising their work)*
Not bad for one day's work.

ALL
Our wall will be the talk of Pau!

ROSE
Two more days, then off to Paris.

ALEX
And a school for Jenny.

HUGO
Didn't Jenny look a picture in that dress?

ALEX
Indeed she did.

GEORGE
So like her mother . . .
Shades of another time . . .
Of vintage nights —
But I digress . . .

(ROSE and ALEX exchange glances. Did he recognize the dress all along? Had he really ever forgotten it? GEORGE offers no explanation, but slowly moves off)

GEORGE *(looking at his watch)*
Good Lord, the time!
Ah well, God bless . . .

(He leaves with JENNY. ALL begin to follow except ROSE and ALEX. A beat. ROSE looks at ALEX)

ROSE
Alex, this has gone on long enough —
What I mean is you and Jenny.

HUGO *(leaving)*
I'll be off now . . .
See you both tomorrow . . .

(He leaves. ROSE continues, more kindly)

ROSE
Since you came, she's truly blossomed —
But, my friend, a flower is fragile . . .
Heaven help you if you hurt her . . .

ALEX
Why all this concern?
God, you're hardly ever here!
Your whole life is your career,
And nothing else matters.

ROSE
My career?
We wouldn't eat if I had no career.
You know that George lost everything.
I do it all for George and Jenny.
I thought you knew that.

ALEX
All right, I'm sorry.

ROSE
Can't you see?
What we three have is something very rare.
In a word, it's happiness.
Nothing in the world will ever
Tear apart the sweet existence
We have spent a lifetime building!

ALEX
Rose, let me explain to you . . .
Yes, I can't deny the feelings that I have . . .
But what's wrong with that?

(He breaks off. How to convince her?)

Rose, I'd never harm the girl . . .

ROSE
You were once prepared to do
A lot of harm to me . . .

ALEX
You cannot compare
This with our insane affair . . .
What I wanted from you
Was both body and soul . . .

ROSE
Aren't you trying to play
An identical role?

ALEX *(face to face)*
This is one thing that I *will* control.

(Dissolves to . . .)

SCENE 11

(The Pyrenees. ALEX retraces with JENNY the journey he first made with ROSE)

JENNY
Do you remember the first time you fell in love?
Did it make you happy or sad?
Did you waste away and lie awake all night?

ALEX
Yes, I remember . . .
I cannot forget . . .
It's haunted my life since then . . .

(A pause. Both remain lost in thought, then, not without calculation:)

JENNY
'Pas de tendresse
Et pas de joie,
Loin d'ici,
Loin de toi.

Rien de plus triste
Que mes soupirs,
Lorsque vient le jour
Où il me faut partir . . .'

(ALEX is moved, only now recognizing the melody)

ALEX
How do you know that?

JENNY
Mummy used to sing it to me.
That was her love song.
Her very first love song . . .

(She turns and looks at him)

Love,
Love changes everything:
How you feel and
What you do . . .

What . . .
What would you say to me,
If I told you
I loved you . . . ?

ALEX *(with difficulty)*
Then I'd have to say to you:
You are bright and sweet and foolish...
Yes, love,
Love changes everything,
But not always
For the best —
Love can sometimes
Be a most
Unwelcome guest...

JENNY
You don't believe that.
You know you're fooling yourself.
Why not be honest?

(moving closer)

Alex,
Be honest...

(She kisses him on the mouth. He allows the kiss to happen. Dissolve to...)

SCENE 12

(In the middle of the night. A room in the house. GEORGE discovered typing)

GEORGE *(to himself, as he types)*
'...Beluga caviar...
My finest vintage champagne...
And then a night of dance...
My ashes to be scattered
among the vines at sunset...'

(ROSE enters, knows immediately what he is doing and interrupts)

ROSE
Oh, do stop planning your wake!
You're bound to outlive us all!

GEORGE *(with a twinkle)*
'... My funeral oration to be written by
Giulietta Trapani...'

(then, suddenly serious, looks up)

Rose, we should talk —
I've got something on my mind.
It's Jenny,
Jenny and Alex —
The whole thing's unnatural
For a girl of her age...

ROSE
You needn't be anxious:
He's explained all this.
And she's no longer a child.
It's just that he's younger
And you're getting jealous.
Am I right?
Anyway, I'm filming in Paris,
And it's her birthday —
We promised we would take her to the
circus —
George, you know that I'm right.

GEORGE
Maybe you're right...
Look, you're free to keep your lover
And your noisy Paris clique.
A man who's pushing eighty
Is not exactly chic...
But Jenny's all I have now —
Don't let *him* take her from me...

ROSE
My darling George, I love you!
How dramatic can you be!

GEORGE
You think that I'm dramatic?
Wait.
If we don't take some action,
We'll be too late...

SCENE 13

(A circus in Paris. JENNY's 15th birthday. The performance is in full swing. We see GEORGE, ROSE, ALEX and JENNY and at the same time they show that they are themselves watching.

We are greeted by a whirlwind of activity: clowns, jugglers, tumblers perform under the streamers and gaudy lights. Various of the CIRCUS PERFORMERS, led by a CHANTEUSE in exaggerated make-up and costume, strike up a song as an accompaniment — part hymn in praise of daring, part invitation for a volunteer from the audience.

At certain points the CHANTEUSE has the CIRCUS AUDIENCE joining in with the song).

CHORUS
Take the journey of a lifetime!
It's only just a drum-roll away!
On the journey of a lifetime
Every day's a high-wire day!

CHANTEUSE
If you've got what it takes,
The stars and streamers are yours!
Take a risk in the ring
And feel the thrill of applause!

(Drum-roll. A KNIFE-THROWER appears and with his ASSISTANT enters the ring. Applause)

If you reach
For the moon,
If you aim
For the sky,
Then the moon
And the sky
Can be yours —
Come on and try!

There's a prize
To be won
Take a risk,
Take a ride,
Right this way,
Have a go,
Try your luck —
And step inside!

If you reach
For the moon,
If you aim
For the sky,
Then the moon
And the sky,
Can be yours —
Come on and try!

(A volunteer is now being sought for the KNIFE-THROWER's act. Attention focuses on JENNY and ALEX, seated side by side. She asks him to step forward, and when eventually he does, it is much to the annoyance of GEORGE. ALEX is led away by the ASSISTANT)

CHORUS
Take the journey of a lifetime!
It's only just a drum-roll away!
On the journey of a lifetime
Every day's a high-wire day!

CHANTEUSE
If you've got what it takes,
The stars and streamers are yours!
Take a risk in the ring
And win the thrill of applause!

(ALEX now reappears clad in a sequined circus jacket. He takes up his position and duly braves the hail of knives. The trick is greeted with great approval by all but GEORGE, who is evidently becoming increasingly distressed by JENNY's obsession for his nephew. As the applause fades the song starts up once again).

CHANTEUSE
If you reach
For the moon,
If you aim
For the sky,
Then the moon
And the sky,
Can be yours —
Come on and try!

There's a prize
To be won,
Take a risk,
Take a ride,
Right this way,
Have a go,
Try your luck —
And step inside!

(ALEX re-emerges, removing his costume. Grinning, he returns to his seat, where he is greeted with an ecstatic embrace from JENNY. The next act is now arriving. JENNY and ALEX are whispering and laughing together. Finally losing his temper, GEORGE breaks in:)

GEORGE
I came to watch a circus
Not an overgrown child!
So either watch the circus
Or just leave us in peace!

ROSE
Don't get moody.
You were young once.
Take no notice.

JENNY
We weren't doing anything. We were only talking.

ALEX
I'd better go.

(to JENNY)

I'll come and see you later.

(leaving)

Enjoy the show...

(JENNY gazes after him)

JENNY
Why's he leaving?

(to GEORGE)

You made him go...

After all, I am fifteen...

(Dissolve to...)

SCENE 14

(Bare stage. ALEX, JENNY, ROSE and
GEORGE are singled out in the darkness. At some
points they sing separately, at some points together,
but throughout they do not acknowledge each other's
presence)

ALEX
Love, and your
World can become
A madhouse.
Love and your
World can become
A circus.
Love turns around . . .

Jenny, your
Love is a
Drug that I dare
Not take, a
Drug to make me mad . . .

Rose, I'd never
Harm the girl . . .

JENNY
Love

Has turned my
World around,
And my
World now turns round
Alex . . .

ROSE
Love should not
Be used as a weapon.
Why, Alex,
Why can't you
See it's George you're . . . ?

ALEX, JENNY & ROSE
Breaking
And burning . . .

Breaking
And bleeding . . .

In the name of
Love . . .

ALEX, JENNY, ROSE & GEORGE
And I'm falling,
I am suddenly falling,
And my story
Is older than the stars . . .

ALEX, JENNY & ROSE
Suddenly falling,
I can feel myself falling . . .
Down into this
Madhouse
Of love . . .

(Dissolve to . . .)

GEORGE
Love is a
Knife. It's a curse.
A cancer.
To love is to
Hate letting
Go . . .
Jenny, I can
Never share your
Love . . .

Suddenly falling,
I can feel myself falling
In this
Madhouse of
Love . . .

SCENE 15

(JENNY's bedroom, GEORGE's Paris flat. Later the same night. ALEX discovered saying his promised goodnight to JENNY)

ALEX
Come on, Jenny.
That's enough now.
Jenny, even mermaids
Have to sleep.

JENNY
I am a mermaid
With golden hair . . .

ALEX
Come on, Jenny.
Be a good girl.

JENNY *(suddenly serious)*
Alex, let me hold you . . .
There's so much I want to say . . .

(She opens the covers. ALEX tentatively gets into bed beside her)

I want you here for ever,
In my arms and in my life,
To belong to you entirely . . .
You know we're not just cousins . . .

ALEX *(getting up)*
We *are* just cousins, Jenny,
And you're fifteen years old.

JENNY *(pulling him back)*
It's not as if I don't know passion
From living in our house . . .
I've learnt that feelings can run deep . . .

ALEX
We'll talk tomorrow —
Go to sleep.

(Passing of time. JENNY is now asleep. ALEX contemplates returning to JENNY's side)

Taking more . . .
Than I ought to take . . .

(snapping out of his rêverie)

What are you doing?
Don't even think it . . .
You have no right to feel this way,
And yet . . .
I love her, and I *must* not love her . . .
I wish to God we'd never met . . .
She ought to be
The last one I should think of . . .

(We have become aware of GEORGE climbing the stairs)

GEORGE
I know he's
Up there with her now . . .

ALEX
She ought to be
The last one I should love . . .

GEORGE
If he is,
My God, I'll kill him . . .

ALEX
She ought to be
The last one I should care for . . .

GEORGE
I should have
Stopped this long ago . . .

ALEX
The very last . . .

(In turmoil, ALEX breaks off. GEORGE meanwhile has begun to make his way across the landing towards JENNY's bedroom, increasingly agitated)

GEORGE
Selfish little cradle-snatcher . . .
Twisted, rotten, heartless monster . . .
Filthy, filthy, callous bastard . . .

(He reaches the bedroom door, breathless. ALEX freezes, hearing GEORGE outside the door)

I was right . . .
He's in there . . .
There he is . . .
He's in there . . .
Jenny, my Jenny,
I can't let him take you,
I . . .

(Surprised by his weakness, he staggers a pace, attempts to regain himself, then suddenly collapses to the floor. ALEX hears the noise and opens the bedroom door. He sees GEORGE's body and immediately stoops down to examine it. He attempts to revive it. In vain)

ALEX
George . . . George . . .
This is *my* fault . . .
All of this is *my* fault . . .

(ROSE and HUGO, both in dressing gowns, now appear from ROSE's bedroom)

ALEX
I was saying goodnight to Jenny.
When I heard a noise in the passage . . .

(looking down at the body)

He must have fallen
And had a heart attack.

HUGO *(to ROSE who is bending down to attempt to revive GEORGE)*
No, it's hopeless . . .

ROSE
He was listening —
Jenny mustn't know.
If she asks you,
Say he died while sitting by the fire —
Help me to move him in there.

(As they start to move the body, JENNY appears in the doorway. The OTHERS turn to look at her, but no one can speak. Dissolve to . . .)

SCENE 16

(Farmland around Pau. A large gathering at GEORGE's wake. GIULIETTA addresses the assembled company which includes ALEX, JENNY, ROSE, MARCEL and an odd mixture of estate workers and GEORGE's famous friends)

GIULIETTA
George was an original man.
He did not want to change human life.
He rejoiced in the way we are made.
He did not look forward to heaven —
He was happy with the earth.
He loved and understood

The flesh, food, wine, love . . .
He lived for today and firmly believed:

If death were given a voice,
That voice would scream through the sky:
Live while you may for I am coming . . .

So . . .

Hand me the wine and the dice,
I want my carnival now,
While I have thirst and lust for living!

So gather all you can reap,
Before you're under the plough —
The hand of death is unforgiving!

Hand me the wine and the dice,
While there are grapes on the vine —
Life is a round of endless pleasures!

The end is always in sight,
But it tastes better with wine —
Why pour your life in tiny measures?

Hand me the wine and the dice,
The time is racing away —
There's not a taste that's not worth trying!

And if tomorrow it ends,
I won't have wasted today —
I will have lived when I am dying!

(ROSE now addresses the assembled throng, clasping in her hands the urn holding GEORGE's ashes)

ROSE
Dear friends and neighbours . . . If what I am doing seems strange to you, I must remind you that I am carrying out the wishes of my husband. He made me promise to strew his ashes among the vines he loved. He asked that everyone should drink his wine, that there should be music and dancing . . .

(The guests are led away by Rose and an impromptu dance begins. JENNY and ALEX appear on the edge of the throng)

ALEX
Why don't you dance with me?

JENNY *(turning away)*
How can you think of dancing?

ALEX
George used to say: you can have more than one emotion at the same time. The one makes the other more acute and then it cures it.

(The dance begins in earnest, becoming increasingly wild and bacchanalian)

GIULIETTA & CHORUS
Hand me the wine and the dice,
While there are grapes on the vine —
Life is a round of endless pleasures!

The end is always in sight,
But it tastes better with wine —
Why pour your life in tiny measures?

Hand me the wine and the dice,
I want my carnival now,
While I have thirst and lust for living!

So gather all you can reap,
Before you're under the plough —
The hand of death is unforgiving!

(ALEX and GIULIETTA finally meet in the midst of the dance)

GIULIETTA
You must be the famous Alex!

ALEX
You must be Giulietta!

GIULIETTA
Tell me, are you still shooting women?

CHORUS
Hand me the wine and the dice!

ALEX
Rose never could keep a secret.

GIULIETTA
Rose and I hide nothing.

ALEX
I heard you got on well together . . .

GIULIETTA
Death says: live while you may, for I am
coming! Do you dance with women of your
own age?

*(He whirls her into the dance, which is now reaching
its frenzied climax, swirling, almost dangerous)*

CHORUS
Hand me the wine and the dice,
The time is racing away —
There's not a taste that's not worth trying!

And if tomorrow it ends,
I won't have wasted today —
I will have lived when I am dying!

*(GIULIETTA and ALEX leave the dance. ROSE
breaks down in tears and rushes away)*

CHORUS
Hand me the wine and the dice,
I want my carnival now,
While I have thirst and lust for living!

So gather all you can reap,
Before you're under the plough —
Life is a round
Of flesh, food, wine, love . . .

*(GIULIETTA and ALEX are strolling together
some way off)*

ALEX *(a little drunk)*
Got the feeling George is watching us —
Only he could make a wake this joyous!
Let's go back and try a tango!

GIULIETTA
Later.
Don't you think a quiet stroll
Would be a little more inviting?

ALEX
Your idea sounds far more promising —
There's a barn that George was fond of
sketching.
Take my word:
You ought to see it . . .

*(He is interrupted by GIULIETTA's kiss. Slightly
stunned, he returns her kiss, they leave together; from
the shadows the figure of Jenny emerges, following
them. Dissolve to . . .)*

SCENE 17

*(The deserted vineyard. ROSE has returned to the
scene of the wake, still crying. HUGO has been
trying to comfort her)*

HUGO
Don't cry, Rose.
You'll always have wonderful memories.

ROSE
Hugo, go away.
Leave me alone.
I mean it.

*(At a loss, he shrugs. MARCEL arrives and urges
HUGO to leave them alone. HUGO departs)*

MARCEL
George would have been so proud of you!
The bravest thing you've done!
Tonight was a wonder!
You're a wonder . . .

(ROSE sobs convulsively)

Rose, you mustn't cry like this.
George would not have wanted that . . .

ROSE
Oh God, I miss him so . . .

MARCEL
Come on, show me a smile . . .

*(Together they walk slowly back into the house.
Dissolve to . . .)*

SCENE 18

*(A hayloft in the barn. Nearly dawn. GIULIETTA
and ALEX lying in the hay. She is startled by a noise.
In the darkness the figure of JENNY retreats and
disappears down the ladder)*

GIULIETTA
What was that?

ALEX *(sitting up)*
What?

GIULIETTA
There.
Listen.

ALEX *(gets up and looks around)*
There's nothing here. I suppose it must have
been a rat.

GIULIETTA
So what do you propose to do, then?
Get married while she's still at school?
Tell her now.
Don't be cruel.

ALEX
There has to be a way to say it . . .
Common sense can be so cold . . .

GIULIETTA
Common sense
Says: be bold.

ALEX
Yes, it's a crime to make her love me —
But surely, it's just as bad to leave her . . .
And yet, that can be the only answer —
The whole damn thing's got out of hand . . .

GIULIETTA
The only crime that I'm aware of
Would be to let our moment die —
Tell her now.
Tell her why.

'A memory of a happy moment,
That's what this time will one day be' —
Tell her that.
Then you're free.

ALEX
Will you still be here when I get back?

GIULIETTA
Yes. But don't be too long, Alex. Don't be too
long.

(He goes. Dissolve to . . .)

SCENE 19

(Outside the house. Dawn. A huge trestle-table
strewn with party debris. JENNY and ALEX alone.
He has broken the news of his departure)

ALEX
Jenny, this is just as hard for me . . .
What we feel is wrong . . .
Unnatural . . .
Our bodies must not rule our minds . . .
You're much too young to understand your
feelings . . .
Can't you see?
This has to finish . . .

JENNY
All right, I heard you.
Now please be quiet.
This needs some thinking.

ALEX
When you're older you will thank me . . .
Come on, Jenny . . .
Little mermaid . . .

JENNY
You say that it's unnatural.
What exactly does that mean?
When you first met my mother
You were only seventeen.
The thing that is unnatural
Is to keep your feelings in.
And lying to yourself must
Be by far the greatest sin.
Oh yes, it's all too easy
To pretend I don't exist . . .

ALEX
Oh Jenny, can't you see that
There are things we must resist?

(She cuts him short)

JENNY
Look, I think I know the reason
You're so keen for this to end —
I saw what you were doing
With your new Italian 'friend'.
You're the one who seems to
Let your body rule your mind.
If that's what being grown-up means,
Then please leave me behind.

ALEX
If my body really ruled me,
Then we both know all too well
You'd end up with a lover
Locked inside a prison cell . . .

JENNY
No one said that Romeo
Was a monster —
Why are you?
I'm as old as Juliet . . .
What . . .
What are you frightened of?
When you know . . .
You know you love me . . .
And love,
Love changes everything,
Turns the tide back,
Breaks the rules . . .

ALEX
Jenny, we're behaving like a pair of fools . . .

JENNY
Are you going to marry her?
Giulietta . . .
Have you said?

(Alex cannot reply)

Because . . .
If you don't marry her . . .
Would you marry me instead?

(by now openly crying)

Why . . .
Why can't you wait for me . . . ?
Three years is not a lifetime . . .

(She cannot continue. ROSE appears in the doorway)

ROSE (to JENNY, quietly)
Darling, I just need a moment . . .
I must have a word with Alex . . .

(JENNY runs away into the garden. ROSE
approaches and pours wine for herself and ALEX)

I hear you're leaving us . . .
Our lives are changing yet again . . .
I came to say goodbye . . .
Good luck . . .
Come back and see us now and then . . .

(She hands a glass to him)

Anything but lonely,
Anything but empty rooms.
There's so much in life to share —
What's the sense when no one else is there?

Anything but lonely,
Anything but only me.
Quiet years in too much space:
That's the thing that's hard to face,
And . . .

You have a right to go,
But you should also know
That I won't be alone for long.

Long days with nothing said
Are not what lie ahead —
I'm sorry, but I'm not that strong . . .

Anything but lonely,
Anything but passing time.
Lonely's what I'll never be,
While there's still some life in me,
And . . .

I'm still young, don't forget,
It isn't over yet —
So many hearts for me to thrill.

If you're not here to say
How good I look each day,
I'll have to find someone who will . . .

Anything but lonely,
Anything but empty rooms.
There's so much in life to share —
What's the sense when no one else is
there . . . ?

(He replaces his glass on the table and moves away)

Just promise one thing . . .

ALEX
All right.
What is it?

ROSE
Don't ask me questions . . .
You must promise first . . .

ALEX
I can't
I must know what it is.

ROSE
Don't leave me!

(JENNY reappears. ALEX turns and leaves them.
JENNY rushes to her mother and they embrace and go
into the house.)

GIULIETTA appears and sits at the table. ALEX
re-enters. They look at one another)

GIULIETTA
It won't be long
Before Jenny's a woman.
What then?

(No reply)

'Hand me the wine and the dice' . . .

(They move towards one another)

BOTH
Love will never,
Never let you
Be the same . . .

ALEX
Love will never,
Never let you
Be the same!

(They embrace again)

END OF ACT TWO

Creative Team

CREATIVE TEAM

Music	ANDREW LLOYD WEBBER
Lyrics	DON BLACK
	CHARLES HART
Based on the novel by	DAVID GARNETT
Director	TREVOR NUNN
Production designer	MARIA BJØRNSON
Lighting	ANDREW BRIDGE
Sound	MARTIN LEVAN
Production musical director	MICHAEL REED
Orchestrations	ANDREW LLOYD WEBBER
	DAVID CULLEN
Choreographer	GILLIAN LYNNE

PRODUCTION TEAM

Assistant to Mr Nunn	ANDREW MACBEAN
Assistant to Miss Lynne	JOHN THORNTON
Assistant to Miss Bjørnson	GUY NICHOLSON
Assistant to Mr Bridges	HUGH VANSTONE
Assistant to Mr Levan	MIKE CLAYTON
Design Co-ordinator	WILL BOWEN
Costume Co-ordinator	SUE WILMINGTON
Costume Supervisor	IRENE BOHAN
Props Supervisor	GABRIELLE BRIDGES
Production Manager	MARTYN HAYES, FOR MARTYN HAYES ASSOCIATES
Assistant Production Manager	MARTIN HEAP
Company Manager	TREVOR WILLIAMSON
Production Stage Manager	ALAN HATTON
Stage Manager	RICHARD ORIEL
Deputy Stage Manager	JOHN BIRGER
Assistant Stage Managers	ROS ATKINSON
	KITTY ETTINGER
Sound Operator	GRAHAM CARMICHAEL
Console Operators	ALAN MATHIESON
	TERENCE ELDRIDGE
Wardrobe Mistress	LYNDA SOUTHON
Wig Supervisor	WENDY FARRIER

ORCHESTRA

Conductor	MICHAEL REED
Leader	ROLF WILSON
Violin	DAVID RANDALL
Viola	DONALD McVAY
Cello	ROBERT BAILEY
Bass	MICHAEL BRITTAIN
Harp	JOHN MARSON
Flute/Piccolo/Alto Flute	ANTHEA COX
Oboe/Cor anglais	JOSEPHINE LIVELY
Clarinet/Bass Clarinet	LESLIE CRAVEN
Saxophone/Clarinet/Flute	JOHN FRANCHI
Horn	DAVID LEE
Piano/Celeste	GEOFFREY EALES
Keyboards	MICHAEL DIXON
Percussion	IAN CHOPPING
Assistant Musical Director	MICHAEL DIXON

THE ORIGINAL CAST

ROSE VIBERT an actress	ANN CRUMB
ALEX DILLINGHAM a young Englishman	MICHAEL BALL
GEORGE DILLINGHAM Alex's uncle, an English painter	KEVIN COLSON
GIULIETTA TRAPANI an Italian sculptress	KATHLEEN ROWE McALLEN
MARCEL RICHARD an actor manager	PAUL BENTLEY
JENNY DILLINGHAM daughter of Rose & George	age 12 ZOE HART
	age 14 DIANA MORRISON
ELIZABETH George's housekeeper	LAUREL FORD
HUGO LE MEUNIER Rose's admirer	DAVID GREER
A circus CHANTEUSE	SALLY SMITH

At the café

Actors	GEOFFREY ABBOTT, JOHN BARR, TIM NILSSON-PAGE, MICHAEL SADLER, SANDY STRALLEN
Actresses	CAROL DUFFY, SUSIE FENWICK, SALLY SMITH

At the fairground

1st Barker	DAVID OAKLEY
2nd Barker	JOHN BARR
Alex's friends	DAVID GREER, MICHAEL SADLER
Their girlfriends	CAROL DUFFY, SUSIE FENWICK
Alex's date	TRILBY HARRIS

In Giulietta's studio

Gondolier	JOHN BARR
Hotel cashier	CAROL DUFFY
Nun	SUSIE FENWICK
Doctor	TIM NILSSON-PAGE
Hotelier	DAVID OAKLEY
Pharmacist	SALLY SMITH

In Rose's dressing room

Friend of Marcel	TIM NILSSON-PAGE
Rose's friends	GEOFFREY ABBOTT, LAUREL FORD, TRILBY HARRIS, DAVID OAKLEY, MICHAEL SADLER, SALLY SMITH

Building a wall

Labourers	GEOFFREY ABBOTT, JOHN BARR, TIM NILSSON-PAGE, DAVID OAKLEY, MICHAEL SADLER, SANDY STRALLEN

At the circus

Clowns	GEOFFREY ABBOTT, TIM NILSSON-PAGE, SANDY STRALLEN
Knife thrower	JOHN BARR
His assistant	TRILBY HARRIS
Trapeze artists	CAROL DUFFY, SUSIE FENWICK

At the wake

The young peasant	SANDY STRALLEN
ALL OTHER PARTS ARE PLAYED BY THE ENSEMBLE	
'Parlez-vous français?' vocal	PETER REEVES
Swings	PATRICK CLANCY, LINDA JARVIS

In the stage production, the role of the younger Jenny was originated by Zoe Hart.

The action takes place in France and Italy between 1947 and 1964. All characters are French unless otherwise stated.

Acknowledgements

The author and publishers are grateful to the production team of *Aspects of Love*, led by Andrew Lloyd Webber, and including Trevor Nunn, Gillian Lynne, Maria Bjørnson, Andrew Bridge, Martin Levan, Don Black and Charles Hart; to Biddy Hayward, Trevor Jackson, Edward Windsor, Bob Eady, Harry Dagnall and Anne Simpson of the Really Useful Theatre Company; to Martyn Hayes, Martin Heap and Alan Hatton from Martyn Hayes Associates; to Sue Wilmingon, for her invaluable help with the costume photography, and Trevor Williamson, the company manager; to Ros Atkinson, Kitty Ettinger, John Birger and Richard Oriel from stage-management; to David Crosswaite for his assistance; and to everyone at the Prince of Wales Theatre for their help.

Special thanks go to the Garnett family, particularly to Jane and Richard Garnett for their hospitality, and to Richard for his patience in answering a never-ending stream of questions and for allowing his archives to be photographed by John Summerhayes; and to Henrietta Garnett for permission to reproduce paintings from the estate of Duncan Grant (pp.16, 17 (top)).

The Charleston Trust at Charleston Farmhouse, Near Firle, Lewes, East Sussex, BN8 6LL (Tel. Ripe (032 183)265) was most helpful. Charleston was the home of Duncan Grant and Vanessa Bell and the focus for many Bloomsbury people.

Thanks are also due to Tony and Frances Bradshaw and Jane Hill of the Bloomsbury Gallery; Christine Geoffrey; Jane Pritchard of the Ballet Rambert Archives; Richard Shone; and in France to Lilian Altar from Roger Viollet, Paris; Panasonic FX120; Pau Golf Club; Taxi du Lagoin, Pau; and Pierre Truchi of the Département du Tourisme.

The publishers are grateful to the following copyright holders for permission to reproduce illustrations: The Charleston Trust, Sussex, p.16 (bottom); Chatto & Windus Ltd, London, pp.18, 19, 20, 21 (top), 28, 29, 32 (top); David Crosswaite, London, p.118; Département du Tourisme, Pau, p.45 (V. Dubourg/Geronis of Pau), p.49 (top); Anthony d'Offay Gallery, London, p.17 (top); Kurt Gänzl, pp.44 (top), 46 and 47 (bottom) (both P. Flery/Y. Prout); the Estate of David Garnett, pp.6, 8, 14, 17 (bottom), 19, 20, 21 (bottom), 23, 24, 25, 27 (bottom); Oliver Garnett, pp.10, 11; Richard Garnett, pp.13, 15, 27 (top); Musée National du Château de Pau, p.44 (bottom); National Portrait Gallery, London, p.16 (top); Pau Golf Club, Pau, p.49; Rambert Dance Company, London, pp.35, 36, 37, 38 (photographs on pp.37 and 38 by Duncan Melvin); Sotheby's, London, pp.39, 40 (Cecil Beaton photographs courtesy of Sotheby's); Thames Television, London, pp.41, 42; Topham Picture Source, London, p.32 (bottom); Roger Viollet, Paris, pp.47 (top), 53.